Alaska's
PRINCE WILLIAM
SOUND

A TRAVELER'S GUIDE

MARYBETH HOLLEMAN

ALASKA NORTHWEST BOOKS™

For Prince William Sound,
for my son James, and for the future of both

ACKNOWLEDGMENTS—I thank those who have spent time in the Sound with me, especially Andy Holleman, with whom I first experienced the place. For manuscript review and technical assistance, thanks to Bob Armstrong, Bob Behrends, Nancy Bird, Sandy Frost, Herman Griese, Peter Haeussler, Tom Hamilton, John F. C. Johnson, Gretchen Legler, Craig Matkin, Marti Miller, Chuck Monnett, Chuck and Rita O'Clair, Perry and Lois Salmonson, and Chris Waythomas. Special thanks to Rick Steiner for helping with this book throughout the process. Most of all, thanks to Prince William Sound for being.

Text © 2000 by Marybeth Holleman
Book compilation © 2000 by Alaska Northwest Books™
An imprint of Graphic Arts Center Publishing Company
P.O. Box 10306, Portland, Oregon 97296-0306, 503-226-2402
www.gacpc.com

Library of Congress Cataloging-in-Publication Data
Holleman, Marybeth.
    Alaska's Prince William Sound / by Marybeth Holleman.
        p. cm. — (An Alaska pocket guide)
    Includes bibliographical references (p.).
    ISBN 0-88240-529-2 (alk. paper)
    1. Natural history—Alaska—Prince William Sound. 2. Prince William
Sound (Alaska)—History. I. Title. II. Series.

QH105.A4 H66 2000
508.798'3—dc21   99-055661
                                                           CIP

PHOTOS—*Front cover:* Yale Arm, © Jeff Gnass; *Back cover:* Cordova Harbor, © Kathryn R. Hough; *Pages 1–2, 95–96:* Lupines, © John Fowler; *Page 3:* Sea otter, © Alissa Crandall; *Page 5:* Barry Arm, © Randy Brandon.

The quote on page 75 is from John Muir's *Edward Henry Harriman*, Point Reyes, Calif.: Coastal Parks Association, 1978, pp. 4–5.

President/Publisher: Charles M. Hopkins
Editorial Staff: Douglas A. Pfeiffer, Ellen Harkins Wheat, Timothy W. Frew, Tricia Brown, Jean Andrews, Alicia I. Paulson, Julia Warren
Production Staff: Richard L. Owsiany, Susan Dupere
Designer: Constance Bollen, cb graphics
Copy Editor: Linda Gunnarson
Map Artist: Gray Mouse Graphics

Printed on acid- and elemental-chlorine-free recycled paper in the United States of America

Contents

INTRODUCTION
The Enchanted Circle

The vast shifting panorama of sea and islands and wooded shores and towering peaks spread before us on every hand....We were afloat in an enchanted circle; we sailed over magic seas under magic skies; we played hide and seek with winter in lucid sunshine over blue and emerald waters.

—John Burroughs, *Harriman Alaska Expedition*

John Burroughs saw Prince William Sound for the first time in 1899. A century later the Sound is still an enchanted circle of mountains, ice fields, and islands within which lies an unmatched diversity of life; it is a place of convergence and magic.

During the summer of 1987, the Sound captivated me so completely that I moved to Alaska. I wanted more time to explore its waters and fjords. That same summer, a man told me, "I could spend many lifetimes exploring Prince William Sound and still not see it all." I think he's right; I come here every year, and still it surprises and charms.

Prince William Sound lies at the apex of the bend in the North Pacific coastline where the Arctic to the north, Aleutians to the west, and Inside Passage to the south all intersect. It is one of the

Rugged shoreline along Orca Inlet leads to the Rude River delta.

———■———

most active seismic regions in the world: the 1964 earthquake centered in the Sound spread its effects farther than any North American earthquake ever recorded. The Sound is encircled by three mountain ranges that feature the sharp ruggedness of geologic youth—the Kenai, Chugach, and St. Elias. Among the peaks that range from 4,000 to 14,000 feet lies the most extensive system of valley glaciers and the largest ice fields in North America.

Prince William Sound forms a circling eddy off the mainstream of Alaska's coastal current. This westward-moving current carries some of the most biologically productive waters in the world, as nutrients and long summer daylight hours create vast blooms of plankton that swirl around the bend of the Gulf of Alaska and into Prince William Sound by way of Hinchinbrook Entrance. Here, water circulates spirally rather than passing straight through, creating a counterclockwise gyre in the center. This gyre, in conjunction with the ice discharged from tidewater glaciers and the hundreds of freshwater streams feeding the Sound, makes this body of water a unique fjord-estuary.

As the water currents circle through, the Aleutian low-pressure system and the North Pacific high pressure system intermingle. Precipitation is high but locally variable: a beach on Montague Island might get 80 inches a year, while an upland forest 5 miles away might receive 300 inches a year. Valdez, located at the end of a long, narrow fjord, holds the world record for snowfall at sea level: 557 inches in 1989–90.

As climates converge, northern temperate and subarctic environmental conditions overlap. Prince William Sound is the northernmost reach of the temperate rain forest, containing some of the largest protected old-growth stands of this forest type left in all the world. In this narrow coastal strip of forest, fragile because of its slow growth rate at northern latitude, the water quality of the hundreds of streams is high, providing spawning grounds for thousands of silver, pink, red, and chum salmon.

Located on the southeastern edge of the Sound is the Copper River Delta, the largest contiguous wetland on the Pacific Coast. From late April to early May, more than 20 million migrating birds

© Randy Brandon

The Sound is an intricate web of land and water.

pass through the delta, creating the greatest concentration of birds in the world. Also in abundance are species that are rare or locally extinct elsewhere; the numbers of bald eagles in Prince William Sound exceed their total population in the Lower 48 states. Threatened species, from humpback and fin whales to Steller sea lions, marbled murrelets, and short-tailed albatross, find an abundance of food and make this place home.

This bounty has also attracted humans for thousands of years. All of the major Native groups in Alaska—Eskimo, Athabascan, Aleut, and Northwest Coast—have lived or traded in this region. Russian fur traders as well as English and Spanish explorers searching for the Northwest Passage sailed into the Sound. In recent times, people have converged in search of quick riches, and their activities mirror the boom-and-bust events of the rest of Alaska. In the early 1900s, the Sound was the approach to the largest copper mine in the world. In the 1970s, it became the land terminus of the longest oil pipeline in the world—the trans-Alaska pipeline—which carries the United States' largest oil supply. In 1989, the Sound was the location of the most damaging oil spill in history.

Exploitation of the "Last Frontier" has played out against threats to the fragile coastal forest and the unique wildlife. Recovery from the oil spill continues to be slow; clearcut logging, especially along eastern Prince William Sound, has damaged the narrow band of coastal rain forest, and perhaps the longest running environmental battle in our nation's history continues over resource development across the Copper River Delta.

Deer cabbage adds fall color to a mountain meadow.

© John Fowler

© Steve Moffitt

Hikers enjoy a magnificent view of Harriman Glacier.

In this book, I include the Copper River Delta with Prince William Sound because it is an integral part of this marine-centered ecosystem. I focus on aspects of Prince William Sound that make it unlike anywhere else in the world, that drew me to stay, and that prompted Burroughs to call it "magic." It's my hope that this book enhances your enjoyment and awareness of Prince William Sound, for as the poet Gary Snyder says, it's those who "learn the flowers" of a particular place who develop a true relationship with the natural world. As you learn the "flowers" of the Sound, I know that you, too, will want this wondrous circle to remain wild and enchanted, so that in another hundred years John Burroughs's words will still ring true. ■

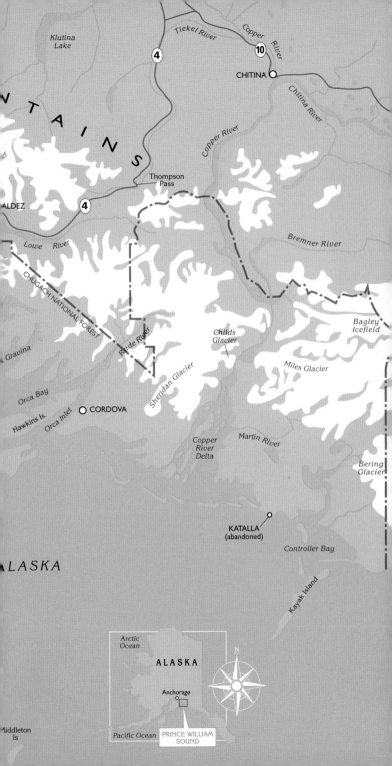

At a Glance

Prince William Sound lies within the Chugach National Forest, at 5.6 million acres the country's second-largest national forest. It's also one of the first to be created in the nation. After visiting Prince William Sound in 1904, W. A. Langille, supervisor of the Tongass National Forest, recommended it for National Forest status. In 1907, President Theodore Roosevelt designated 4.9 million acres as the Chugach National Forest. Two years later, Roosevelt added the Bering and Copper River Deltas.

With the passage of the 1980 Alaska National Interest Lands Conservation Act, 2 million acres of northwestern Prince William Sound were set aside as the Nellie Juan/College Fiord Wilderness Study Area, to be studied for future wilderness designation. Also at that time, a congressional mandate established the Copper River Delta as the only Forest Service area in the nation to be managed primarily for fish and wildlife protection.

The Chugach is arguably the nation's wildest forest—it's 98 percent roadless—but it still has no official wilderness designations. The Forest Service is presently revising the Chugach National Forest management plan, and it's expected that many areas will be recommended for wilderness and wild river status.

While most land along the Sound is part of the Chugach National Forest, thousands of acres are owned by Alaska Native

Kayakers enjoy a close, quiet encounter in Blackstone Bay.

Fishers cast for salmon along Orca Inlet.

corporations and the State of Alaska. These lands were selected from the National Forest under the terms of the Alaska Statehood Act of 1958 and the Alaska Native Claims Settlement Act of 1971.

Location: 60 degrees latitude; in Southcentral Alaska, 60 miles east of Anchorage, 300 miles northwest of Juneau.

Size: 10,000 square miles, about the size of Puget Sound. More than 3,500 miles of heavily convoluted shoreline, more than 150 glaciers, 34 major islands, and hundreds of smaller islands. Over 30 percent of the Chugach National Forest is covered by glaciers.

USGS topo maps: Seward, Cordova, Valdez, Anchorage, Blying Sound.

Weather: Prince William Sound has a maritime climate of moderate temperatures, high humidity, extreme precipitation, and frequent overcast and fog. Summer temperatures usually range from 40° to 60°F, with some 70°F days. Winter temperatures range from −20° to 40°F. Precipitation averages 200 inches, about half falling as snow in winter. In summer, rain may fall two-thirds of the time; April, May, and June are the driest months, with September and October the wettest.

Winds: While Montague and Hinchinbrook Islands protect the Sound from the Gulf of Alaska's high seas, winds can build to more than 100 miles per hour. When winds are funneled through mountain passes or down fjords, they pick up significantly. Rough seas and strong tidal currents can create dangerous conditions. There are also local gusty winds called "williwaws."

Surface water temperatures: By August, water temperatures in protected coves can reach 55°F but are usually lower. Throughout fall, winter, and spring, water temperatures range from 30° to 40°F. Immersion without a wetsuit will cause hypothermia (loss of body heat) within minutes and can be fatal.

Access: By highway at Valdez (305 miles from Anchorage) and—beginning in summer 2000—at Whittier (60 miles from

© Kathryn R. Hough

© Marybeth Holleman

Beached icebergs along Barry Arm delight the author's son.

Anchorage). In summer, the Alaska Railroad makes one daily trip from Anchorage to Whittier, and several a day between Portage and Whittier. The Alaska State Ferry system makes stops at Chenega Bay, Whittier, Valdez, and Cordova. Both the Portage-to-Whittier train and the state ferry carry cars and RVs. There are regularly scheduled commercial flights to Cordova and Valdez, as well as air-taxi service out of Anchorage. All train, ferry, and plane schedules are reduced in winter.

Facilities: Valdez and Cordova have an array of lodging; Whittier has a couple of small hotels. The Chugach National Forest rents 23 public-use cabins that must be reserved in advance. Backcountry camping is allowed on all Forest Service lands. City

HOW TO TREAT THE SOUND

As JOHN BURROUGHS WROTE a century ago, "Two things constantly baffle and mislead the eye in all these Alaska waters—size and distance." Prince William Sound's vastness can create dangerous conditions, so if you venture onto it, you must be prepared. And, while it is vast, it's also finite and fragile, and as more and more of us explore its still-wild waters, we need to protect that wildness for both ourselves and its wild inhabitants.

■ File a trip plan with family, friends, the harbormaster, and the outfitter. Take along extra food, warm clothing, high-quality water-proof rain gear, extra fuel, and tarps. Carry and use navigational charts, a tidebook, a VHF marine radio, and emergency locator gear.

■ Stay at least 1/4 mile away from the face of any tidewater glacier. Calving ice and resulting waves can flip boats. Keep back from icebergs as well; they can break apart or roll suddenly. Beware of underwater moraines where waters become shallow quickly, such as at Blackstone Bay and Unakwik Inlet. Don't climb on either tidewater or land glaciers unless you're experienced and prepared for falling ice and deep crevasses.

■ Keep a respectful distance from wildlife. Watching animals should not prompt a change in their behavior. It is illegal to harass or

campgrounds with RV sites are available in Valdez, Cordova, and Whittier.

Visitor information: Cordova Chamber of Commerce: P.O. Box 99, Cordova, AK 99574; 907/424-7260. Valdez Convention and Visitors Bureau: P.O. Box 1603, Valdez, AK 99686; 800/770-5954. Whittier Chamber of Commerce: P.O. Box 607, Whittier, AK 99693; 907/472-2309.

Scenic flights: Trips over the Columbia Glacier, Copper River Delta, and other glaciers and fjords are available through charters departing from Anchorage, Cordova, and Valdez.

State ferry: A popular loop trip from Anchorage is to drive to Portage, take the train to Whittier, ride the ferry from Whittier

---

disturb any marine mammal. Keep at least 100 yards away and limit your time to 1/2 hour. Don't chase whales or porpoises. Instead, cut your engine and let them decide whether they want to approach you.

- Follow developed trails. Don't hack shrubs or trees. When hiking off the trail across muskeg meadows, spread out. Going single file can kill fragile wetland plants.

- If you come upon an archaeological site, leave artifacts alone. Report the site to the Forest Service, or the Chugach Heritage Foundation at 907/561-3143.

- Respect others' wilderness experiences. Reduce wake when passing other boaters; avoid beaching or camping near others.

- Leave no trace of your visit. Camp on beaches above high tide, not in fragile meadows or near beach-nesting birds. Use campstoves or fire pans, but if you must have a beach fire, build it below high-tide line, keep it small, and use only downed wood. Wash on beaches, away from tidepools and streams. Defecate in tide zones or dig a hole away from fresh water and bury it; burn or pack out used toilet paper. Completely burn all trash to prevent bear encounters; pack out what you can't burn. Disassemble any fire rings, tent sites, etc., from your visit before leaving. Clean up after others. ■

Visitors are dwarfed by the face of Shoup Glacier.

across the Sound to Valdez, and then drive from Valdez back to Anchorage via the scenic Richardson and Glenn Highways.

Boat tours: Many companies operate out of Whittier, Valdez, and Cordova. Some specialize in glacier trips; others offer whale-watching trips. Scheduled trips range from a few hours to a couple of days; custom trips are also available. Cruise ships visit the Sound after traveling up Southeast Alaska's Inside Passage.

Private boating: Many explore the Sound in their own seaworthy sailboats and motorboats, but they must be knowledge-able of weather and sea conditions as well as safe anchorages in the Sound's deep fjords.

Kayaking: Prince William Sound's protected waters make kayaking appealing. But the waters are cold and the wilderness remote, so preparation and trip planning, along with local information, are essential for inexperienced paddlers. Kayak instruction, guides, and rentals are available in Anchorage, Whittier, Valdez, and Cordova. Floatplanes provide drop-offs and pick-ups out of Whittier and Valdez. Some, such as the Prince William Sound Kayak Center, offer both kayaks and water-taxi service.

Fishing: Both saltwater and freshwater. There are plenty of runs of silver, pink, and red salmon in the Sound, as well as good fishing for king salmon, halibut, red snapper, Dolly Varden, and cutthroat trout. Charters are available for daylong trips, but you can also fish from shore in Whittier, Valdez, and Cordova. Alaska sportfishing licenses, available at most sporting goods stores, are required for fishing anywhere on the Sound.

Hiking: There are a few established trails around Whittier, Valdez, and Cordova, but along the rest of the Sound it's necessary to bushwhack. Some places are so dense it's nearly impossible, but ridges near glaciers and islands with muskeg meadows make for inviting hikes up to high points with grand views. Avoid damaging fragile plant life and be prepared for bear encounters, mosquito clouds, and changing weather.

River rafting: Out of Cordova, rafting on the Sheridan and Copper Rivers, and from Valdez, through Keystone Canyon on the Lowe River.

Bird viewing: More than 200 species of birds, including seabird rookeries and spring shorebird migrations, especially on the Copper River Delta.

Beachcombing: Especially on the sandy outer coasts in spring, treasures such as Japanese glass floats can be found.

For more information: Alaska Public Lands Information Center: 907/271-2737. Sound Alliance/NWF: 907/258-4800. Chugach National Forest: 3301 C Street, Suite 300, Anchorage, AK 99503; 907/271-2500. Cordova Ranger District: P.O. Box 280, Cordova, AK 99574; 907/424-7661. Chugach State Parks: 907/345-5014. ■

◄ © Randy Brandon

Rock and Ice

It's the meeting of ice scouring above and tectonic plates colliding below that has created Prince William Sound. The effects of these twin forces aren't yet covered by the green mantle of time, nor have they ended.

When world temperatures dropped several million years ago, snow accumulated on higher peaks and formed ice fields. During major episodes of glaciation, Prince William Sound was completely covered by an ice sheet thousands of feet thick. During the last glaciation 10,000 years ago, the southern tips of Montague and Hinchinbrook Islands and mountain peaks above 2,000 feet remained uncovered. You can tell which mountain peaks rose above the ice: they are jagged, sawtooth ridges. Those that were beneath are rounded, like you see on Perry Island. As tongues of ice poured from mountains, they also scoured out valleys, leaving behind the characteristic U-shape of Alaska's geologically young valleys. Flying over Kings Bay, you can see the U-shaped valley descend into the bay, where it continues under water. The fjords of the Sound are flooded U-shaped valleys, scoured to water depths of hundreds, even thousands, of feet. The deepest inshore spot along the North Pacific coast lies off Lone Island and is 1/2 mile deep.

A column of ice calves off Child's Glacier.

EARTHQUAKE!

ON THE EVENING OF MARCH 27, 1964, the largest recorded quake ever to hit North America shook Prince William Sound. The Pacific Plate lurched under the North American Plate, and an earthquake of magnitude 9.2 shook the earth. Centered 20 miles under Miners Lake, on the peninsula separating College Fiord from Unakwik Inlet, this quake rattled over 500,000 square miles and caused tsunami flooding as far away as Crescent City, California, and Hilo, Hawaii.

The human toll was huge for such a sparsely populated area: nearly 70 lives were lost in Valdez, Whittier, and Chenega. Chenega alone lost a third of its residents; because it was such a small, close-knit Native village, everyone lost family. Both it and Valdez were later relocated. Within the 500-square-mile-wide area hardest hit, including Anchorage, 115 people died and $750 million in property was destroyed.

The quake was the longest ever recorded: shocks lasted 3 to 5 minutes. It caused land to rise and fall—Portage sank below sea level, and Tatitlek's harbor rose above sea level. More devastating were the tsunamis, giant waves caused by submarine landslides that rose up to 200 feet along the shoreline. They washed away buildings, harbors, boats, and people.

The landscape was drastically reshaped. In the northern Sound, the land sank as much as 6 feet, flooding forests with salt water. In the southern sound, the land rose, up to 38 feet on Montague Island, creating new beaches, altering streams, and destroying clam beds, most notably in Orca Inlet. Chenega Island and surrounding areas shifted more than 60 feet south.

Today, if you enter Prince William Sound through Portage, you can see the sunken remains of a few houses. At the old Chenega site on Chenega Island, the only thing visible from the water is the old school-house, standing alone on a grassy hill. Along Passage Canal and most of northwestern Prince William Sound are stands of dead spruce, killed when the land sank below sea level and salt water flowed to their roots. They stand nearly 40 years later as salt-preserved monuments to the earth's powerful forces. ■

Earthquake-destroyed Old Chenega remains off-limits to visitors.

———————◼———————

Meanwhile, beneath the surface, continental plates have been grinding and colliding for more than 40 million years. Prince William Sound lies at one end of the Aleutian Trench, a volcanic "ring of fire" that extends to the Kamchatka Peninsula in Russia. This 2,500-mile-long trench marks the subduction zone where the Pacific Plate slides under the North American Plate. As it slides, the earth heaves and sinks, sometimes slowly, sometimes quickly and violently, as it did during the 1964 earthquake. There's evidence of other earthquakes of equal force. When Captain George Vancouver stopped at Montague Island in 1791, he found that tree stumps cut by Spanish explorer Lieutenant Fidalgo 7 years earlier were submerged even at low tide. Today, dozens of small earthquakes subtly shift the land each year as glaciers continue to sculpt from above.

Prince William Sound's more than 150 glaciers are temperate glaciers—they form and move more quickly than the polar glaciers of Greenland and Antarctica. Dry, cold polar glaciers are frozen to rock and barely move; temperate glaciers have meltwater at their base that acts as a lubricant, allowing them to slide hundreds of feet a year. Polar glaciers also form more slowly. Snow in Antarctica takes hundreds of years to become glacial ice; in Prince William Sound, it takes only a few years.

Most glaciers pour down from ice fields, large level sheets of ice hundreds of feet thick. Four feed Prince William Sound: Sargent

Icefield in the Kenai Mountains pours into the western Sound; Whittier Icefield, much smaller, crowns Passage Canal; Chugach Icefield, made up of many connecting pieces, feeds glaciers from College Fiord to Columbia Glacier; and Bagley Icefield feeds the Copper River and the Gulf of Alaska. Bagley is the birthplace of the largest glacier in the world outside Greenland and Antarctica: the Bering Glacier.

Some glaciers, called cirque glaciers, form from local snow accumulation and are typically wide, thin, and small. Because of their circular erosion pattern, cirque glaciers form beautiful rock basins walled by jagged-edged peaks called arêtes. From the boat harbor in Valdez, you can see a dozen cirque glaciers.

Some ice-field glaciers terminate before reaching seawater. They hang from steep-sided valleys, like Yale Glacier in College Fiord; they pour into a lake, like the Bering; or they end in a broad expanse of braided streams, like Tebenkof Glacier at the mouth of Blackstone Bay. Tebenkof, visible when you come out of Passage Canal into Port Wells, looks like a tidewater glacier from a distance, but up close you can see the dense alder thicket laced with meltwater streams that guards the glacier's face.

It's the tidewater glaciers, those that flow from mountains to sea, that most capture our attention. You can boat up near their massive ice faces and watch the forces of tides and warm air crack the ice, causing it to fall like lightning bolts into the water.

Often you can hear cracks like thunderbolts. Sometimes these emanate from inside the glacier, whose surface is broken into crevasses, stretch marks made as the ice flows down under the force of gravity. Ice falls within these crevasses as well—they can be hundreds of feet deep. But sometimes the thunder comes from the glacier's face, and ice falls in chunks or streams or columns. As it crashes into the water, long waves radiate outward, breaking onto the shoreline and rocking boats and icebergs.

Pure glacial ice is a magnificent crystal blue. It's so dense that it absorbs long wavelengths of light, reflecting only the short wavelengths of blue and green. But not all of the glacier is this pure blue; some is mixed with bits of scoured rock called "glacial flour."

As if released from this crystal blue ice, the skies above glaciers can be clear blue even when the rest of the Sound is wet.

© Randy Brandon

THE MIGHTY COLUMBIA GLACIER RETREATS

FLOWING NEARLY 40 MILES from 13,000-foot peaks to salt water, the Columbia Glacier is one of the fastest moving and biggest in Prince William Sound. At its face, it is more than 3 miles wide and up to 200 feet tall; in the summer of 1999, its rate of flow was clocked at over 114 feet per day. But the mighty giant is shrinking.

As most of the Sound's glaciers retreated over the last hundred years, the Columbia continued to advance and then stabilized. Each winter, it advanced to ride up onto Heather Island, pushing a rocky shoal with its snout. In summer, it retreated off the island. Then, in 1973, an ice-bound lake emptied, and glaciologists predicted a retreat. Sure enough, it now retreats a half-mile a year, shrinking by nearly 9 miles in the past 17 years. Though it's still 15 miles from land, glaciologists predict it will be landlocked within the next century.

Until the last decade, the state ferry and tour boats could motor so close to the glacier's face that it filled the sky. Now, a vast field of icebergs trapped between its face and its old terminal moraine keeps boats at a distance. These icebergs also drift into oil-tanker shipping lanes from Valdez, increasing the risks of collision. The *Exxon Valdez* was avoiding the Columbia's icebergs when it grounded on Bligh Reef.

Some glaciologists suspect that Columbia's retreat—and that of 80 percent of Alaska's more than 1,000 glaciers—may be a sign of global warming. Warmer summers have melted glaciers faster than winter snows build them up, causing them not only to retreat but also to thin at lower elevations. ◼

Kayakers maneuver among a tidewater glacier's cast-off ice.

———————◼———————

Many times I've boated to a glacier under wet, gray skies to be rewarded with clear skies tumbling down the glacier's face and to our boat. This sort of clearing at the glacier's face isn't unusual: glaciers create their own local climates. The high, cold ice fields create high pressure that naturally flows down the glacier to the low pressure in the wet Sound, pushing clouds back.

Most of the Sound's 17 tidewater wonders are on the western side of the Sound. Columbia Glacier, the second-largest after the Bering, is closer to Valdez, but most are more accessible from Whittier. College and Harriman Fiords, off Port Wells in the north-western corner of Prince William Sound, are often called "Glacier Bay of the North" for the glaciers pouring down one after another toward salt water. These glaciers stream from an ice field containing the highest point in the Sound, 13,176-foot Mount Marcus Baker. Where the 2 fjords split off from Port Wells lies Barry Arm, at the end of which lie 3 tidewater glaciers: Barry, Cascade, and Coxe.

As glaciers move forward, they also melt, especially at their terminus. If they melt and calve faster than they move forward, they retreat back up the fjord. For the last few centuries, most of the Sound's glaciers, including Barry, have been retreating. Only a few are still advancing, including Cascade, Coxe, Harvard, and Meares. At the head of Harriman Fiord lies the long, broad face of Harriman Glacier, which advanced for most of the century, so much so that a kittiwake colony abandoned the area in the early 1980s.

At retreating glaciers such as the Nellie Juan and Columbia, and on the rounded rocks of Esther Passage and Perry Island, you'll find evidence of glacial sculpting. On bare, rounded rocks on the east side of Nellie Juan, you can find glacial striations, deep scratches left by rock rubble at the bottom of the retreating glacier. Another mark of the Nellie Juan's retreat over the last hundred years is a long spit, often strewn with a gallery of beached icebergs like sculptures in a museum. Between the spit and the glacier is a long lagoon where harbor seals and black-legged kittiwakes feed on the upwelling of nutrients at the glacier's face.

Nellie Juan's spit is a terminal moraine from which the glacier retreated in 1935. Moraines are thick bands of rock and soil deposited by a glacier. Alongside some glaciers are lateral moraines running down either side of the glacier; sometimes you'll see a medial moraine in the middle, where 2 glaciers have come together like branches of a river. Terminal moraines form at the front, or snout, of the glacier and are pushed forward as the glacier advances and then are left behind when it retreats. Many of these old terminal moraines are now rocky shoals under water, as in Barry Arm, Harriman Fiord, College Fiord, Icy Bay, and Blackstone Bay. In Unakwik Inlet, a terminal moraine rises 750 feet above the sea bottom.

Blackstone Bay's underwater terminal moraine lies off Willard Island; it's estimated that the glaciers retreated from this moraine in about 1350. Now, 2 tidewater glaciers, Blackstone and Beloit, lie at the head of the bay. Both are in retreat and may soon become landlocked like the Tebenkof.

On the Copper River Delta, there are 2 glaciers that calve into a river instead of into the sea: the Miles and Childs Glaciers. At the end of the 50-mile road from Cordova to the Million Dollar Bridge, the Childs Glacier calves into the Copper River, sometimes sending waves crashing on the opposite shore, where a viewing platform now protects visitors from high, dangerously strong waves.

Whichever tidewater glacier you choose to visit, beware: once you drift in front of one and watch ice calve, you, too, may find that nothing else compares to this thunderous evidence of the forces that sculpt the landscape around you. ◼

The Northernmost Rain Forest

One summer, I spent a week at the U.S. Forest Service cabin on Pigot Bay. There with kayaks, a friend, and my 7-year-old son, I looked forward to days of paddling the quiet waters of this small bay.

But it rained. And rained. Day after day, unceasingly. Not just a gentle mist, but a steady pour. We paddled out anyhow, for that's the pact you make when you decide to visit Prince William Sound: come rain or shine. Besides, the wet days only make the sunny ones more beautiful, glistening, and fresh.

On the fourth day, we paddled to a swollen stream that roared through its rocky channel and dropped 10 feet into salt water. In the bay around it, the water was reddish brown from decaying plant material, particularly the needles of spruce and hemlock.

That steady rain carried nutrients from forest to sea, where they fed the bacteria and plankton at the base of the marine food chain. I became thankful for the rain, for I'd gotten to see the rain forest in its truest form—water streaming from every low spot onto the beach, into the sea.

Prince William Sound is the northernmost reach of rain forest in the world. It anchors the northern end of the world's largest contiguous temperate rain forest, which stretches south as far as California's redwoods. With hundreds of inches of rain and snow

Sitka spruce and Western hemlock shade a rainforest stream.

falling each year, the forest literally drips most of the time. Water is the lifeblood of this place.

The cycle of water shapes Prince William Sound. Water in the Gulf of Alaska evaporates. Low-pressure systems circling counter-clockwise cause this moisture to collide with coastal mountains encircling the Sound. As this moisture rises, it cools, condenses, and falls as rain or snow, washing down mountainsides. It filters through the forest and muskeg and then drains back to the sea in streams and creeks and rivers.

Water links land and sea. Rainwater carries nutrients from the forests to the sea by way of more than 3,000 waterways. Salmon return to spawn in more than 2,000 of these, and seabirds return to nest in trees and grassy hummocks, both bringing nutrients back into the forest.

This thin membrane between sea and ice is narrow. Only 15 percent of the Sound's land mass is forested, but it contains great structural diversity: spruce-hemlock forests, shrublands, muskegs, alpine meadows, and rocky peaks.

If you set out to explore this forest, you'll want to wear water-proof boots and be prepared to cautiously make your own way through, keeping an ear tuned for bears. Above the high-tide line along beaches, especially along those facing the Gulf of Alaska, you may find a jumble of driftwood, and then behind it stands of ryegrass or clumps of beach greens growing on gravel. Beyond, the land might dip into a marsh or rise into an alder thicket before becoming forested. Alder thickets can seem impenetrable—they are notoriously right at eye level and grow tangled and thick.

If you stay near the shoreline, you may follow the forest's edge along strikingly beautiful steep cliffs. Here trees cling to nearly bare rock in just the thinnest layer of soil, their roots stretching in all directions. Sculpted by sea storms, they grow lopsided, their branches reaching back into the forest. On the cliffs grow an abundance of plants, including ferns, saxifrage, and the carnivo-rous but lovely butterwort. The rock is nearly always damp, and these plants survive on the nutrients carried in that water.

If you head inland, you'll soon enter a deep forest dominated by Sitka spruce and western hemlock. These two and the

EVERGREENS AT THE EDGE

ALONG PRINCE WILLIAM SOUND, 4 species of evergreen trees grow at their northernmost range along the Pacific: Sitka spruce, western hemlock, mountain hemlock, and Alaska yellow cedar. On the other side of the Chugach, Kenai, and St. Elias Mountains, where it's drier and often colder, black and white spruce predominate. The Sound's evergreens not only require wet, coastal areas but also tolerate salt spray and thin soils by radiating their roots outward to grasp bedrock.

Sitka spruce has been called the most storm-resistant tree in the world. Its form is perfectly adapted to the Sound's environment: it has a flat crown that spills the wind, branches that point slightly downward to shake off snow, and needles as hard as steel that radiate out from all sides of the twigs. Grab a Sitka branch and the needles will prick your hand. Sitka spruce is the largest tree in Alaska, reaching heights of more than 160 feet.

Western hemlock, most abundant in Southeast Alaska but common along the Sound, is most easily identified by the slender leading shoots that droop from the narrow crown and branches, and by the soft, flexible needles. At higher elevations, mountain hemlock is more common, sometimes growing as a shrub in muskegs and as surprisingly large trees on mountain slopes. Western and mountain hemlock interbreed throughout their range. On the Harriman Expedition, John Muir was delighted to find "the only pure forest of mountain hemlock I ever saw" along the Sound, the same "most beautiful evergreens" that he treasured in the High Sierra.

Alaska yellow cedar is the least common of the Sound's evergreens, growing in scattered locations primarily in the eastern Sound. Like hemlock, its crown droops and its needles are flexible, but the shreddy gray bark and scale-like needles forming flattened sprays are characteristic of cedar.

While all 4 species range as far south as northern California, the colder temperatures and weaker sunlight of the Sound slow their growth. It's estimated that it would take these forests up to 400 years to return to climax after windthrow or logging; the same species in Oregon takes less than half that long. ■

A stream tumbles through muskeg and forest toward Port Wells.

less-common Alaska yellow cedar are often festooned with epiphytes—ferns and old man's beard and moss that cling to their bark and live off the rainfall, creating entire plant communities on tree limbs. The trees rise straight and narrow as the towering climax species of the coastal temperate rain forest.

The understory is composed of plants that are either delicious or dangerous. You'll find berry bushes that, ripening in August, bears and birds and humans love—the plump orange salmonberry, waxy purple blueberry, and shiny red currants. But you may also find the large, maple-shaped leaves of devil's club, beneath which lie stems thick with sharp, stinging thorns, or the delicate water hemlock, which looks like the edible cow parsnip but is one of the most poisonous plants known.

The forest floor is carpeted with a deep humus and fallen logs—decomposition happens more slowly here than in rain forests to the south because of lower temperatures, longer winters, and less light. Growing on logs, limbs, and humus are mosses and plants such as the delicate watermelon berry, whose white flowers and red berries alike taste like their namesake. In some low areas near rivers, you may come upon small stands of black cottonwood, one of few deciduous trees in the Sound.

After making your way through the forest, you may find yourself on the edge of a meadow, thinking you've found a good camping spot. But one step onto it tells you otherwise: it's a muskeg, made of thick sphagnum moss that holds water like a sponge. On its soft surface grows an abundance of wildflowers, but in this elfin landscape you must look carefully to see such beauties as bog cranberry, cloudberry, and chocolate lily.

At its edges, you may find a few tenacious mountain hemlocks, dwarfed and distorted like bonsai trees. Their growth stunted by the soggy ground, these trees may be more than 500 years old, though they are only a few inches in diameter and a few feet tall.

You'll often find a series of small, still ponds dotting muskegs, like reflecting pools in a Japanese garden. On larger ones, the yellow butterballs of pond lilies float. Once I found slick trails linking pond to pond in some muskegs and, upon following them, found three river otters playing in a larger pool. They had made the trails, sliding on their bellies from one pond to the next, down the mountainside to the sea.

While not suited for pitching a tent, muskegs do make for easier hiking. On some islands, such as Culross, they're so plentiful that you can muskeg-hop, walking from one to the next, skirting the forest and climbing to stunning views of fjords and islands and glaciers beyond.

If you continue climbing, you'll get above treeline, which is from 1,500 to 2,000 feet in this subarctic alpine zone. Shrub

SKUNK CABBAGE

A PATCH OF SKUNK CABBAGE, named for its pungent, earthy smell, always reminds me I'm in a rain forest. It grows as far south as southern California, but its big leaves stand out in this subarctic forest. Prince William Sound is its northernmost range, where it thrives in swampy woods where the water table is $1\,^1/_2$ feet or less from the surface, growing leaves as long as 6 feet and as wide as $1\,^1/_2$ feet. The bright yellow spathe and spike of tiny flowers shoot up first in spring, a favorite food for bears, deer, and geese after the long winter. ■

THE MINIATURE PLANT WORLD OF THE MUSKEG

As GLACIERS RETREAT, plants colonize bare rock, forming forests after hundreds of years. But where water doesn't drain, a lack of oxygen suffocates growth, limiting nitrogen and phosphorus nutrients and preventing larger plants from taking hold. Instead, a muskeg, or bog, forms.

The pioneer plant of the muskeg is sphagnum moss. It fills ponds with peaty layers, creating muskeg. Eventually, enough layers accumulate to form solid ground. This tassel-headed moss grows thick and deep, changing color with moisture levels, from pale green to bright red. Not only does it hold several times its weight in water, but it is also naturally antiseptic. Wounded animals have been known to lie in it; Natives used it for diapering babies; pioneers chinked cabin logs with it.

Because its color matches the sphagnum, and because it is usually less than 2 inches across, round-leaved sundew (above) is frequently overlooked. But it is worth getting down on all fours to find. In early summer, look for tiny white blossoms on slender stalks arising from a rosette of basal leaves that hug the ground. The round leaves bear tiny red hairs tipped with drops of deadly fluids. Insects mistaking them for dewdrops stick to this bog carnivore. As the hairs curl inward, preventing escape, the fluids slowly digest the insect, providing nutrients to the sundew that the acidic muskeg cannot.

Several fragrant orchids also thrive in these muskegs. Ladies' tresses have tiny, white, tubular flowers arranged spirally. The white bog orchid, or bog candle, looks much like ladies' tresses, except the flowers are flared and not arranged in spirals. The northern green bog orchid is, as its name suggests, nearly identical in appearance to the white orchids except for the color: a camouflaging yellowish green.

If you come upon a muskeg, walk carefully. It's fragile and full of small wonders that will reward your careful, gentle observations with windows onto new landscapes. ■

thickets mark the boundary between forest and alpine. Besides Sitka alder and willow, these thickets contain salmonberry, elderberry, and mountain ash, creating a difficult but beautiful tangle of berries near summer's end, and a feast for many forest birds and mammals. These thickets are also common in disturbed areas such as clearcuts, earthquake uplifts, avalanche chutes, and areas of recent glacial retreat.

Once through the thickets, you'll be rewarded with open alpine country, also called tundra, where an average of 9 months of snow cover makes for a short growing season. Here, low mats of crowberry, dwarf blueberry, and mountain heather predominate. Like the muskegs, this is a land of miniatures. Above tundra are rocky peaks encrusted with lichen, the pioneering plant that breaks down rock into nutrients and soil for other plant life. You'll also find scree slopes, a steep slide of small, loose rocks.

With this diversity of habitat, it's always an adventure walking the forests of the Sound. And each area has its own distinctive features. On Perry Island, for example, hiking is made easy by abundant muskeg and alpine habitat, and a deep-water lake lies at the center of the island. But on any walk through the rain forests of Prince William Sound, you're sure to come upon water—be it muskeg, pond, stream, river, or rain—the lifeblood coursing everywhere, shaping and sustaining. ■

© Marybeth Holleman

False hellebore is beautiful but poisonous.

Land Dwellers

They may live on land, but the 38 species of mammals inhabiting the islands and mainland of Prince William Sound depend on water. Salt water provides a panoply of shelled and finned food. Rain nourishes abundant plants that provide food in summer; it also grows the dense forest canopy that reduces winter snowpack, wind speed, and heat loss. The animals depend on this old-growth rain forest for the mature canopy and its vaulted root systems and cavities, ideal spaces for denning and resting.

The water also isolates: land animals must swim frigid ocean currents or traverse jagged peaks and ice fields to reach new territory. Most often they don't, but sometimes they surprise us. One summer day my friend and I watched an animal swim across Culross Passage from the island to the mainland. It looked too slow and graceless to be a river otter. Finally, a mountain goat emerged and alternately stamped and shook off water and numbness for a half-hour before disappearing up the mountainside to safety.

Another example: in 1973, a young male brown bear that was found raiding garbage cans was transplanted 47 air miles from Cordova to Montague Island. Less than a month later, he was found within 100 yards of where he was caught. Besides the long land journey, the bear had swum 7 miles across open water, including the strong currents of Hinchinbrook Entrance.

The Sound's brown bears can exceed 800 pounds.

OTTERS OF LAND AND SEA

IF YOU SEE A FURRY ANIMAL in the water, you might ask: sea otter or river otter? If it swims on its back, floating like a boat, it's a sea otter. If it swims forward like a beaver, with only its head showing, it's most likely a river otter. Both river and sea otters are excellent swimmers and divers. Members of the weasel family, they both feast on intertidal life: mollusks, crabs, small fish, and urchins. But at Prince William Sound, you're more likely to see sea otters than river otters, which are elusive in their forest cover.

Sea otters are the smallest marine mammal—they're never seen in freshwater and rarely on land, except for hauling out in tidal zones and on ice floes. For warmth, they depend not on blubber but on their fur—at 1 million hairs per square inch, the densest of any animal. Still, they eat up to 25 percent of their 40 to 100 pounds in body weight per day to stay warm. After diving to retrieve food—urchins and crabs are favorites—they float on their backs, using a rock to break shells. Then they use their bellies like tables and wash by rolling in the water. When sleeping, sea otters will lay their heads on one another's bellies or wrap themselves in kelp fronds to keep from drifting to shore. They're highly social and will form rafts of hundreds of animals.

Long and lithe, river otters can swim as far as 18 miles offshore, but are more at home on land. There, they can run as fast as a person, reaching speeds of 15 miles per hour sliding and running down snow and ice. They live in mature forests, denning at the base of old spruce and hemlock, and feed not only on sea creatures but also on small rodents and young birds.

Both sea otters and river otters were once hunted nearly to extinction. Sought by Russian fur traders, sea otters had disappeared from most of the Sound by 1911. A small colony at northern Montague Island survived and spread. River otters, too, were heavily trapped in the early 1900s. By 1930, they were scarce in southwestern Prince William Sound. Both species, but especially sea otters, were crippled by the 1989 oil spill in this same area. Sea otters are now protected through the Marine Mammal Protection Act, but river otters are still trapped with few restrictions. Because they continue to suffer from the oil spill, however, river otter trapping has been more restricted in the southwestern portion of the Sound. ■

Brown bears, the world's largest omnivore, live along the Sound and grow to sizes that rival the Kodiak brown bears. Reaching more than 800 pounds, they are easily distinguishable from the Sound's other resident bear, the black bear. While size isn't a reliable identifier, black bears reach no more than 400 pounds. Brown bears have a hump between the shoulder and a dish-shaped face, while black bears have a straight, "Roman nose" face. It's not color that distinguishes them: black bears can be brown, brown bears can be nearly black. In fact, there's a rare blue phase of the black bear, called the glacier bear, that is found from Prince William Sound south to Juneau.

Location alone will tell you which bear you're seeing around the Sound, for the two occupy distinct territories. Brown bears roam the southern and eastern Sound, notably Hawkins, Hinchinbrook, and Montague Islands, the Copper River Delta, and Gravina and Fidalgo Bays. Black bears inhabit the western and northeastern mainland and all other islands except Perry, Naked, and Green.

Black bears thrive here, where they find deep snow for hibernating and alternating forest and avalanche zones for cover and food. After foraging on emerging vegetation along the snow-melt line in early summer, they feast on salmon at stream mouths and then gorge on berries in late summer. Brown bears also follow this seasonal diet, adding to it small mammals and the eggs and chicks of ducks and geese. They frequent open areas such as alpine landscape and deltas more than the reclusive black bears.

While populations of both black and brown bears are healthy now, increased logging, mining, and human settlement along Prince William Sound can threaten their futures, as they need plenty of uninhabited space. Even remote cabins are a threat because they promote conflicts in which the bear inevitably loses. Brown bear populations on Montague have dropped in part because of conflicts with loggers and deer hunters as well as remote settlements.

The other large mammals of Prince William Sound are herbivores. Mountain goats walk alpine ridges, especially those in the extreme southwestern Sound and from Columbia Glacier to the Copper River Delta. They are most often seen as the moving white dots high on mountainsides.

Sitka black-tailed deer are smaller than white-tailed deer.

Two herbivores are transplants. Moose, translocated to the Copper River Delta between 1948 and 1958, have thrived, gaining more flat shrubland habitat since the 1964 earthquake. Small, naturally occurring moose populations exist in Kings Bay and around Valdez as well.

Between 1918 and 1924, 24 Sitka black-tailed deer were translocated from Sitka to Hawkins and Hinchinbrook Islands, extending their northern reach. Now, about 10,000 deer occupy all the larger islands, their numbers held down by weather and hunting. In winters with deep snow, deer retreat to the shoreline and subsist on kelp. But it's a poor substitute for shrubs and herbs; deer can actually starve with full stomachs. Clearcutting exacerbates matters, diminishing shelter and leaving food buried deeper.

The weasel family is well represented throughout the Sound, including not only the largest family member, sea otters, but also short-tailed weasels (ermines), mink, river otters, martens, and wolverines. The small ermine turns white in winter, except its black-tipped tail—this serves as a foil for predators, which strike at the black hairs and end up with only air. Mink, larger than ermines but smaller than river otters, prey mainly on voles. They demonstrate a twist on the lynx-hare cycle: when vole populations are high, mink remain in the forests. But within a couple of years after vole populations' crash, mink move to the shoreside, where they vie with river otters for crabs and small fish.

In winter, ermines and mink dive into deep snow and "swim" beneath it, as does their prey, the shrew; mink and river otters slide down snowbanks on their bellies. The wolverine, found only on the mainland, seems cumbersome in comparison. Broad-backed and stocky, it is strong and clever, known not only to remove bait and trapped animals, but also to destroy or "hide" the traps. Along with the tree-hopping marten, wolverines are reclusive and move out of areas increasingly used by people.

Least reclusive is the red squirrel, which usually nests in tree hollows and whose most apparent signature is a midden of spruce-cone scales under a favorite feeding stump or branch.

There's quite a bit of difference between the Sound's mainland and island land-animal populations. Many species are found only on the mainland, among them porcupines, lynx, coyotes, snowshoe hares, Alaskan little brown bats, muskrats, and wolves. Some animals venture onto some of the bigger islands; beavers, for example, thrive in the wetlands of the mainland as well as on Hawkins and Hinchinbrook Islands. An animal's adaptations can vary from mainland to island: the hoary marmot dens among alpine boulders and along rock slides on the mainland, but on larger islands it also dens at tideline.

Some scientists believe the islands of the Sound also contain some endemic species found nowhere else in the world: the Montague Island tundra vole, the island red-backed vole, and the orca red-backed vole. These are among the dozen or more different voles, shrews, and lemmings to inhabit different niches along Prince William Sound.

These variations in species distribution and adaptations create distinctly different animal communities across the Sound. They are reminders of the matrix of water—from seawater to rain to ice field—that not only sustains, but also defines, the world of Prince William Sound's land animals. ■

Between High and Low Tide

When we go down to the low tide line, we enter a world that is as old as the earth itself—the primeval meeting place of the elements of earth and water, a place of compromise and conflict and eternal change.

—Rachel Carson, *The Edge of the Sea*

After floating in the sea, they find a hard surface, attach themselves by their heads, and within 12 hours build a volcano-shaped shell around their soft crustacean bodies. When the tide is high, they open a hatch and extend 6 feathery legs that kick food into their mouths. When the tide recedes, they shut tight, sealing in moisture.

Their plain appearance belies the fascinating adaptations of barnacles, one of many minute and complex creatures to inhabit the intertidal zone of Prince William Sound. Life here must survive twice-daily submersion in seawater and exposure to the air. At high tide, intertidal organisms live in the relative stability of the water world, but at low tide they endure extremes of hot and cold, wind, rain, and the drying sun. Many close up to the air, for their food is in the sea. In Prince William Sound, the intertidal zone is shaped by some of the most extreme tides in the world.

Ochre sea stars on sea lettuce are exposed at low tide.

———■———

It's shaped, too, by the Sound's varied shoreline, which provides a range of intertidal habitats. Some are sand beaches and cobblestones where few life forms can cling as the force of waves tumble them. But they can be found: at the high-tide line, turn over a rock, and you're likely to find many small animals hopping about. These beach hoppers, or scuds, are amphipods whose tails act like springboards. They eat plant and animal remains washed up by the tide.

Mud flats are prevalent in protected bays and around stream mouths, such as Picturesque Cove off Culross Passage. Here, the small lagoon drains at low tide, revealing fine mud littered with shells. Life lies below the surface, sticking up tubes into the water to catch oxygen and feed. Bivalves, including butter clams, littleneck clams, and cockles, squirt as you walk by, and you may be tempted to dig some for dinner. But red tide, a toxic algae bloom that contaminates bivalves, is so prevalent that humans risk paralytic shellfish poisoning (PSP) unless they've checked with

▶ © Marybeth Holleman

TIDEPOOL LIFE

AT FIRST GLANCE, you might not see much—maybe the waving arms of eelgrass, the bright green cellophane leaves of sea lettuce, or a pink mat of coralline algae. But look closer. Get on your knees or squat down. Peer into that pool of still water. You'll see small snails camouflaged against the gray rock, moving slowly or not at all. Then something moves quickly, extending spidery legs: a hermit crab. Next you notice the purple arm extending from beneath a clump of sea lettuce: an ochre sea star. And on the side, clinging to vertical rock, a small red flower, a northern red anemone's fragile tentacles reaching for food. A darting motion catches your eye, and you find a small fish, motionless now and mottled to match the rock—a sculpin.

This is tidepool life. It is hidden, sheltered, and quiet, awaiting the next tide's waves to bring the next meal. Each tidepool you peer into will reveal a different collage of color and texture. The tidepools mirror the complexity of Prince William Sound itself—in miniature. ◼

Breadcrumb sponges can harbor small invertebrates.

---◼---

local sources beforehand. Often covering these mud flats like long strands of hair is eelgrass, which reaches 7 feet in length. These slender, green fronds provide cover for snails, hermit crabs, amphipods, blennies, and marine worms.

Rocky shorelines are Prince William Sound's most common shoreline type, as well as the most complex intertidal habitat. Rocky intertidal inhabitants are the main food sources for sea otters, harlequin ducks, scoters, and many other seabirds. Here, myriad creatures cling to bare rock, braving the highs and lows in the open. They are tenacious and plentiful—on many rocks and headlands, every toehold is taken.

Each creature has unique adaptations to protect against the two biggest dangers—being crushed or being swept away by the force of the waves. The barnacle is cemented to the rock, and its shape, like that of the limpet, is conical, best for taking the force of water and shedding it quickly. The limpet adheres like a suction cup: the stronger the force of the wave, the tighter it holds. Sea stars and sea urchins have hundreds of tiny suction feet that also hold them tightly. Most animals have shapes that keep them close to the rock.

Seaweeds often have holdfasts and flexible stipes and blades that give under the force of wave and tide.

Along these rocky shores are horizontal intertidal zones where life forms are sorted according to the amount of dry time they can sustain. The highest tide line is the spray zone. Never submerged, this zone is created by saltwater spray. It's also called the "black zone" for the signature coating of black lichen. At high tide it's the only zone that can be seen, like a black bathtub ring around the Sound.

The upper intertidal zone, submerged briefly around spring tides, is often a white band. It's the territory of acorn barnacles, tiny periwinkle snails, and speckled limpets. In places, green algae coat the rock like splattered paint. Creatures in this zone have hard-shell protection against the drying air and the pounding waves.

THE PULL OF THE MOON

RISING AND FALLING SEAWATER creates the meeting of land and sea at the intertidal zone. In Prince William Sound, these tides are mixed semidiurnal, which means they cycle twice in a 25-hour period. Their ranges follow the cycle of the moon.

As the moon makes its elliptical rotation around the earth every 28 days, its gravity pulls the earth's waters toward it, creating a bulge of water. The earth's centrifugal force creates a lesser bulge on the opposite side. When the moon is at a right angle to the sun, at waxing and waning quarter moons, the sun's gravity partially cancels the moon's gravity, thus causing lower, or "neap" tides. When the moon and sun are aligned, around both full and new moons, their combined gravitational forces make the water spring up higher. This "spring" tide is the time of greatest tidal range, which in the Sound can create 24-foot tidal ranges, one of the greatest in the world.

Along with the pull of the moon, the shape of the body of water affects tidal ranges. So, in funnel-shaped bays and fjords such as those in Prince William Sound, tides can reach higher extremes than along wide, broad stretches of coastline. ◼

Farther down is the middle intertidal zone, often a dense band of Pacific blue mussels punctuated with clusters of rockweed, a brown-orange seaweed also known as popweed for the sound it makes if stepped on at ebb tide. The blue mussel, the most abundant mollusk in the Sound, attaches itself to the rock by strong threads secreted from a gland at the base of its foot. (It, too, while edible, may carry PSP.) Beneath this interwoven mat of mussels and popweed are dog whelks, shield limpets, and black chitons. Also called gumboot, the chiton is a prized food among coastal Natives.

At the lower middle zone, some creatures from the lower inter-tidal zone venture up in search of prey. Clinging to rock faces and within cracks may be sea urchins or the carnivorous Aleutian moon snail, found only in Alaska. Ochre sea stars, which range from brown to purple to yellow, often cling to vertical rock, hiding from the drying sun until they can prey on mussels in the safety of seawater. While these are the most commonly seen, an abundance of different sea stars prey in the Sound's middle and lower intertidal zones, including sun stars, leather stars, mottled stars, 24-armed sunflower stars, and brittle stars.

The lower intertidal zone, sometimes called the kelp zone, is briefly uncovered during spring low tides. In the Sound, this zone has the greatest diversity. Here plant life abounds, and animals often lack the hard shells of the barnacle zone because they live submerged most of the time. Kelp forests wave, sea cucumbers and red and green anemone filter-feed, and the giant chiton—at a foot long, the largest chiton in the world—grazes. Green sea urchins, a favored food of sea otters, also thrive here. When sea otters were driven near extinction, many kelp beds in the Sound were heavily grazed by a burgeoning green sea urchin population. Here, too, the giant octopus sometimes ventures. In Alaska, this octopus grows only to about 40 pounds; the largest ever caught, off the coast of British Columbia, was 600 pounds.

If you schedule your trip to Prince William Sound to coincide with "spring" tides, you can explore this lowest zone. As a marine biologist once told me, if you want to see what lives here, you have to put your face where your boot is. ■

Life Beneath the Waves

One July, a friend and I were heading back from Perry Island to Whittier in higher than usual seas for our 15-foot inflatable boat. Sitting in the bow, I kept my eyes glued to the horizon as the waves bounced us. Then, off to the right, a Steller sea lion rose in the water and looked at me. He tossed a silver salmon high into the air, caught it in his mouth, turned on his side, and disappeared. His brief but joyous appearance reminded me that an abundant and diverse world lies below the water's surface.

In the spring, as the days lengthen, the smallest and the largest of the Sound's marine inhabitants return. Feeding on nutrients stirred up by winter's storms, microscopic phytoplankton bloom in huge numbers, producing 80 percent of the entire ocean's oxygen and providing the base of the Sound's food chain, and massive humpback whales return to feed on the abundance of krill, small shrimplike zooplankton swept into the Sound from the Gulf.

Nearly 100 humpbacks spend summers in the Sound. Some stay year-round, but most migrate up from southern wintering grounds in May and then depart again in August. These massive whales, which can reach 60 feet long and 35 tons, arrive hungry. All winter, in the bays of the Hawaiian Islands or Sea of Cortez, they rarely eat, relying on blubber built up in the summer. Having lost up

Steller sea lions congregate on the Needle.

A humpback whale shows its fluke.

---

to a third of their weight, they come to the Sound to feast on krill and small fish. They strain prey through the coarse, brushlike strips—baleen—that hang from the roofs of their mouths. Eating up to 2 tons a day, they build up a 3- to 4-inch layer of blubber for the fall migration.

While known for their complex and melodic songs, these whales don't seem to sing in the summer. You're most likely to find them in the passages of southwestern Prince William Sound from May through August; in the past few years, more have been spotted in the Sound. After several blows, they raise their flukes (tails) for deep dives that can last nearly 30 minutes. Biologists identify individuals by the white and black markings on the undersides of their flukes. They have been listed as endangered since 1966, when whaling had reduced the world's population to 1,000. Now, the North Pacific is home to about 2,000 of the estimated worldwide population of 10,000.

All of the Sound's marine mammals are protected in U.S. waters under the Marine Mammal Protection Act, but some, like the minke whale, are still commercially harvested elsewhere. The minke, which also spends summers in the Sound, is the smallest baleen whale in the North Pacific. A fast swimmer, it has a sharply pointed head and doesn't show its fluke upon diving. One sighting of a large, black back with a small dorsal fin is usually all you see of the shy minke. Less frequently seen is the larger fin whale, which is also black with small dorsal fins, but generally prefers the deeper waters of the Gulf of Alaska.

Gray whales may be spotted along the outer coast of the Sound in spring and fall as they migrate between summer feeding areas in the Bering, Chukchi, and Beaufort Seas and winter calving grounds in Baja California. Sperm whales, the largest of the toothed whales, stay in the deeper waters of the Gulf of Alaska and are rarely spotted along the outer coasts. But there are exceptions: a pilot once saw 3 sperm whales, 2 smaller than the third, off Orca Narrows near Cordova during a long and extreme midwinter storm. A few weeks later, the body of a sperm whale was found washed up on Esther Island. Its size—52 feet long—and well-worn teeth suggested it was at least 50 years old. Marine biologists think the younger whales were escorting the older whale into quiet waters to die.

Prince William Sound does have a few year-round resident cetaceans. Orcas, or killer whales, are often seen in groups of only a few to pods of more than 20. Their smaller cousins, the Dall porpoise and harbor porpoise, frequent bays and fjords. Dall porpoises, found only in the North Pacific, have black and white markings that have earned them the nickname "little killer whales"; except for their much smaller size, they may be mistaken for orcas. I made that mistake the first time I saw them. Paddling across Blackstone in still waters and a soft rain, I suddenly heard a loud *pffft* close to my kayak. I heard another and then glimpsed a black and white dorsal. "Killer whale!" I thought, paddling faster. But then I saw another and realized it was too small and fast to be an orca. It was a pod of curious Dall porpoises.

The friendly Dall porpoises are frequent bow riders, slicing the waters in front of a boat, crossing under the bow, and racing at speeds of up to 30 mph for as long as a half-hour. They may well be the fastest marine mammal. In contrast, the harbor porpoise is shy and moves in slow arcs through the water. Alaska's smallest cetacean, this dark gray to brown porpoise stays at the edges of bays, inlets, fjords, and river mouths where the waters are less than 300 feet deep.

Sea otters, the smallest marine mammal and largest member of the weasel family, are frequently seen in shallow waters. You may also spot a harbor seal swimming quietly in a lagoon, or a few hauled out on ice in front of tidewater glaciers. Because harbor seals spend half their time out of water, these icebergs, as well as intertidal areas where they can let the incoming tide rise around them, provide easy haul-outs in protected waters. They're often confused with Steller sea

DISAPPEARANCES

IN THE LAST FEW DECADES, Steller sea lions and harbor seals have nearly disappeared from the waters of Prince William Sound. The number of Steller sea lions, largest of North American carnivores, has fallen by more than 75 percent in 40 years, adding them to the endangered species list in 1990. Harbor seals, too, are dwindling: in 20 years, their numbers have fallen by 80 percent.

What's going on? While many factors may contribute, from El Niño to contaminant buildup, most now agree that an inadequate food source is literally causing these animals to starve. Half of the sea lion's diet is walleye pollock, the same fish that constitutes the biggest single-species commercial fishery in the world, a fishery that has been booming since the early 1970s. In addition, seabirds that rely on pollock, such as common murres, are also losing ground. All indications point to nutritional deficiency, from thinning egg shells and thinner breast plates in seabirds, to anemic and smaller sea lions and seals.

Exclusion zones around sea lion rookeries and the timing of fisheries to avoid critical times of year for these species may help alleviate the problem. Many agree, though, that greater restrictions on fisheries are necessary, both to prevent disturbance and to assure adequate food sources for the animals. ■

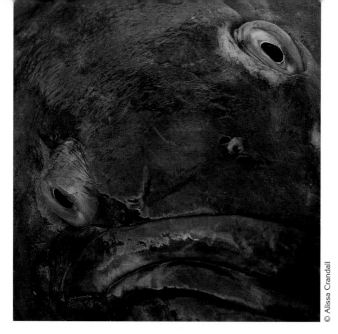

The Pacific halibut is one of the Sound's most proficient predators.

lions, but are smaller, with mottled coloration. In the water, Stellers swim in groups with their noses up, and slap a flipper before diving, while harbor seals, usually swimming alone with their noses forward, quietly sink, noses last. Stellers also prefer more rugged outer-island haul-outs; one of the largest congregations of Stellers left in the Sound is at the Needle in Montague Strait, although you're most likely to see them on buoy markers in channels.

The Sound also has an abundance of fish upon which these marine mammals feed. Foot-long Pacific herring are the bread and butter of the marine food web in the Sound. In March and April, in schools of a million or more, these fast fish with silver underbellies and blue backs migrate from deeper waters to inter-tidal areas, where they turn hundreds of miles of shoreline milky white from the milt released by males spawning in seaweed. Gulls, eagles, and ravens, as well as seals, sea lions, and even humpbacks, gather to feed on the converging fish and their eggs. If they're not eaten, or dried by the outgoing tide, surviving eggs stick to seaweed, eelgrass, and even rocks.

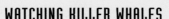

WATCHING KILLER WHALES

"THERE'S ZAIKOF," says Eva Saulitis. "He's shy; see how he always gets behind another whale? It makes it hard to get a photo of him." Saulitis and Craig Matkin are bouncing along in an aluminum skiff beside a pod of killer whales, the most frequently seen whales in the Sound. They identify individual whales as easily as we identify friends. For the past 17 years, Matkin has been studying the orcas of Prince William Sound through photo identification: he and Saulitis photograph dorsal fins, which, along with the shape of the white saddle patch and various scratches and notches, identify individuals like fingerprints.

Their work shows that, of the more than 300 orcas who frequent the Sound, there are 2 distinct populations: residents and transients. Residents form maternal family groups that travel in pods of 6 to 40 whales and eat only fish, preferring silver and king salmon. Matkin and Saulitis have watched many times as resident orcas dove into a school of pink salmon and came up with the errant silver. Transients, which generally travel in groups of less than 7, are predators of harbor seals, Dall porpoises, even humpback whales.

Amazingly, other marine mammals seem to know the difference between the two types of orcas. At the Needle in southwestern Prince

The Sound also has many anadromous fish—fish that spend time in both fresh and salt water. Besides 5 species of salmon, which begin and end their lives in freshwater, there are Dolly Varden and cutthroat trout. Dollies, named after a female character in a Charles Dickens novel with a pink spotted dress, range all along Alaska's coast, spending their first few years in streams, then spending summers at sea and winters in lakes. They can reach 25 inches in length. The cutthroat trout, named for the bright red slash under its jaw, can spend its entire life in streams or lakes, but some migrate out to sea to feed between May and July, then return to freshwater to overwinter. Prince William Sound is the northwestern limit of their range.

William Sound, sea lions don't change their behavior when resident pods pass, but crowd up higher on the rocks, barking and acting agitated, when transients come hunting. And, one summer, a Dall porpoise actually swam with a resident orca pod, even though transients regularly prey on porpoises.

While at the top of the food chain in the Sound, these 20- to 30-foot toothed whales have suffered at the hands of humans. In the mid-1980s, one resident pod learned to take black cod from long lines as the fishers pulled them up. This led some fishers to shoot at the whales in attempts to dissuade them. Several whales turned up dead. The 1989 oil spill has done even more harm to the orcas of the Sound.

In the past few years, resident pods have spent more time in Resurrection Bay outside Seward than in the Sound. One reason may be the lingering effects of the spill. Another may be their preference for silver and king salmon: while Prince William Sound has been stocked primarily with pinks, Resurrection Bay has been stocked with silvers and kings.

Most recently, Matkin and Saulitis have been documenting the buildup of contaminants such as DDT and PCB in the Sound's orcas and educating the increasing number of tour boat operators on how to refrain from harassment while whale watching. ■

Rockfish—from the black sea bass to the red snapper—may look distasteful with their bulging eyes and spiny fins, but they are considered by many locals to be the tastiest fish in the Sound. These stout fish are among the longest lived of all fish, some reaching 100 years. They're also unusual among fish because they bear their young live rather than laying eggs.

The largest, most valuable flatfish in the North Pacific, the Pacific halibut begins life as a 1/3-inch-long larva drifting with ocean currents, one of millions hatched from a single female's egg pool. When it's still less than an inch long, its left eye migrates and its mouth contorts to the right. At 4 to 6 inches, it weighs enough to settle to the ocean floor, where it feeds on fish and invertebrates.

AMAZING PACIFIC SALMON

FIVE OF THE SIX TYPES of Pacific salmon swim the waters of Prince William Sound; all but one spawn here. Born in freshwater streams, they develop in gravel beds as alevins—egg-sac fry—until spring, when most swim to the sea to spend their adult lives. All return to their natal stream to spawn, their color and shape changing as they reenter freshwater; all die within days of laying and fertilizing eggs.

The smallest and most abundant are the pink salmon, also called "humpies" because the male's back distorts into a hump when spawning. Most pinks spawn in the intertidal reaches of the Sound's streams, rather than struggling up steep streambeds like other species. Their life span of 2 years is the shortest of any salmon. Pinks return to spawn in more than 900 stream mouths and 5 hatcheries in late summer.

Chum salmon, also named "dog salmon" because they were traditionally fed to dog teams, have a 4- to 5-year life cycle. Weighing 8 to 10 pounds, they're the second most abundant species, spawning in about 100 of the Sound's streams.

Sockeye salmon are also called "red salmon" for the color they turn when they enter freshwater. When spawning, like a pink, the male's back forms a hump and its jaws become crooked; its head also turns bright green. There are fewer sockeye in the Sound because they spawn in lakes, but they inhabit Coghill, Eshamy, and Miners Lakes in the northwestern Sound. Reds live from 4 to 6 years and weigh 6 to 15 pounds.

Silver, or coho, salmon juveniles spend at least 1 year in freshwater. The last to return each year, the 3- to 4-year-old adults spawn from August through November. At least 25 streams in the Sound contain silvers; the Copper and Bering Rivers' runs of silvers are among the largest on the Pacific Coast.

The King, or chinook, salmon is Alaska's state fish, and the largest salmon at 10 to 120 pounds. While they don't spawn in the Sound, some "feeder kings" come in following the herring between October and June. Kings spawn at 4 to 7 years of age. ◼

As it grows, it heads for deeper waters, but returns to shallow bays and inlets to feed on salmon runs. Living nearly 50 years, these fish can weigh several hundred pounds. The state record is 440 pounds, but there have been unverified reports of

10-foot-long, 700-pound behemoths. When reeled in, these strong-tailed fish can thrash enough to sink small boats and injure people.

While not known as shark-infested waters, Prince William Sound does host a few species of sharks during summer months. The spiny dogfish, or sand shark, reaches 6 feet in length and scavenges the ocean floor. Less often found in shallower waters are the powerful salmon sharks, and in the deepest waters are the Pacific sleeper sharks, which eat squid, seals, and octopus and can reach 25 feet in length.

Sharing the bottom with halibut and sharks are many sea flora, such as the giant cup sponge, which divers have found large enough to sit in. Among these underwater seaweeds and sponges are commercially important dungeness, tanner, and king crabs. Several species of shrimp—the prawn-sized spots and coonstripes and the cocktail humpies and pinks—thrive in coveted "holes" throughout the Sound.

Drifting among the vast blooms of phytoplankton and larval phases of sea stars, halibut, and herring are many otherworldly animals. During winter, before plankton blooms arrive, the water is much clearer and you can see farther into it. Paddling in a quiet lagoon along Green Island one March, I noticed delicate, pink petals waving gracefully among kelp fronds about 20 feet under water. On shore, I found one, stranded—an inch-long melibe, or nudibranch, translucent and formless out of its element.

There are also 2 kinds of jellyfish in the Sound: the small, white, saucer-shaped moon jellyfish and the larger, poisonous, orange-red lion's mane jellyfish. At the head of Eshamy one June day, I saw dozens of lion's mane jellyfish, some up to 2 feet in diameter with 50-foot-long tentacles, floating like an underwater flower garden. These jellyfish are among the largest in the world and float in waters from Point Barrow to southern California.

Because most of us only glimpse this watery world from the narrow band of the surface, it's difficult to know how our actions above affect the vast world below. But they do—as history has shown time and again. Beneath the waves lies the very heart of Prince William Sound, complex and vital, and when one of its inhabitants makes a surface appearance, we are all the more enriched. ■

Winging It Through the Seasons

I f you're a bird watcher, there's no finer place to be than on the waters of Prince William Sound in spring. Especially on the vast tidal flats of the Copper River Delta, you can be surrounded by thousands of birds feeding in one of the world's richest coastal environments before continuing their long journeys.

But even if you're not a birder, it's impossible not to notice birds on Prince William Sound. About half of Alaska's currently known 456 bird species spend time here. Of these, more than 100 are year-round residents; the rest pass through in spring and fall, come from the south for the summer, or come from the north for the winter. It's a cycle in which every season finds a different mix of birds.

Another reason it's hard to miss seeing birds on the Sound is that about half are water birds. Larger and more conspicuous than forest birds, they spend much of their time in the open. These include shorebirds such as black oystercatchers and dunlins, waterfowl such as colorful harlequin ducks and scoters, and alcids—seabirds that spend winters on the open ocean—such as the bright-beaked puffins and penguin-like pigeon guillemots.

Birds that are rare in other parts of the country are also plentiful here. The bald eagle, one of the largest and most

Bald eagles nest in old-growth trees along the Sound's shores.

◀ © Alissa Crandall

frequently seen birds in the Sound, is more abundant in Alaska than anywhere else in the United States; an estimated 6,000 individuals spend time here, some occupying the same nests for decades. The bald eagle was the only species to recover from the 1989 oil spill in the first 10 years.

Less noticeable, but one of the most abundant birds in the Sound, is the marbled murrelet, a small alcid federally listed as threatened in the Pacific Northwest because its old-growth forest nesting sites are disappearing. These small, mottled brown birds bob in high seas and fly at more than 100 miles per hour through dense forests.

The Sound is also host to the Aleutian tern, which can be seen only in Alaska. It nests primarily on the Copper River Delta. These supreme fliers disappear out to sea in August, their wintering grounds unknown.

Their cousins, the more abundant arctic terns, are among the first arrivals in spring and the first to leave in fall, making the longest migration of any animal—more than 12,000 miles to the southern tip of South America. They nest on beaches and in tideland meadows, laying their speckled eggs on gravel for camouflage. Like others who nest in the open, they fiercely protect their nests.

Boating at Barry Arm in northwestern Prince William Sound, I once watched a dozen angry terns chase a bald eagle away from their rookery, where a fuzzy chick was making its first tentative swim. The eagle aimed for the chick, but the adults dive-bombed and screeched so fearlessly and tirelessly that, though the eagle was five times as large as a single tern, it finally retreated, escorted by the agile terns like a cloud of mosquitoes after a caribou.

The terns' springtime return heralds an end to the long months of quiet winter. In late April, the forests ring with hundreds of thousands of thrushes, warblers, and sparrows migrating through tundra and forest. In the marshes and tide zones, millions of waterfowl and shorebirds alight to rest and feed on aquatic life, and the skies fill with swallows. The birds' long and carefully timed journeys are rewarded with Alaska's long summer daylight, which accelerates food production and enhances breeding behavior. This seemingly endless stream occurs in only a few weeks.

In summer, the forests are filled with birds. A regular camp visitor is the Steller jay, a striking bird with a blue body blending into a black head, crowned with a crest of feathers like a punk haircut. When Georg Wilhelm Steller, the Russian naturalist who traveled with Captain Vitus Bering, documented this bird on Kayak Island in 1741, he knew they had landed in North America, for he had seen drawings of blue jays from a book on the Carolinas.

TRUMPETER SWANS

© Marybeth Holleman

THE WORLD'S LARGEST WATERFOWL, the trumpeter swan was considered nearly extinct until 1954, when approximately 3,000 were discovered on the Copper River Delta. Since then, the Alaska population has increased fivefold, and at least half of these 16,000 swans congregate on the delta's Martin and Bering Lakes in spring and fall to prepare for migration.

These birds, which average 25 pounds and have 6- to 10-foot wingspans, are known to live 30 years. They mate for life and maintain strong bonds not only with mates but also with nesting territory— shallow ponds with plenty of nesting material and water plants for feeding. While most head south for the winter, about 50 swans have begun spending winters on Eyak Lake outside Cordova, where a small area at the lake's outlet remains ice-free. ■

Camp visitors may also include Alaska's smallest bird, the rufous hummingbird. One tour operator says that dozens visit his feeder off his floating lodge each summer. Hummingbirds also frequent a feeder at the Harrison Lagoon U.S. Forest Service cabin. One June, two of the tiny birds ended up in the cabin after we left the door open, buzzing around the feeder's window. My son and I gently caught them, cupping them in both hands, and released them outside.

It's shorebirds and seabirds that you'll most notice in summer. In the vast Sound, they all find their niche for nesting and feeding. Prince William Sound contains nearly a dozen large cliff-nesting colonies that house thousands of birds. Some, like the kittiwake

THE GREAT SPRING MIGRATION

colony across from Whittier, are composed of one predominant species. Others, like Wooded Island off Montague Island, provide nesting sites for many. Fifteen different species nest on this one island, including parakeet auklets, Leach's storm petrels, common murres, and pelagic cormorants. Nests of predators—ravens, bald eagles, and peregrine falcons—are nearby.

While kittiwakes, murres, and cormorants nest on steep cliffs, other birds nest in rocky crevasses or earthen holes within grassy hummocks atop islets, like the pigeon guillemot colony in the middle of Jackpot Bay. Tufted and horned puffins and petrels burrow in grassy hummocks, sometimes atop steep cliffs where other birds nest, though petrels nest only along the outer coastline.

IN SPRING, MORE THAN 20 MILLION birds fly through Prince William Sound and the Copper River Delta, one of the most important nesting and staging areas in North America. The numbers are astonishing. Biologists have counted 250,000 shorebirds congregating per square mile, 50,000 red phalaropes rafting in Hinchinbrook Entrance, and 5,500 pintails and 500 whistling swans passing overhead every hour. The 1989 oil spill, beginning right before the great spring migration, killed more than 700,000 birds.

Why so many birds in the same place at the same time? This far north, the short breeding season requires birds to arrive at nesting grounds as soon as the ice is out and plant growth begins. The northern arc of the Gulf of Alaska and the steep, rugged, glacier-filled coastal mountains along much of the outer coastline funnel them along a narrow coastal route through Prince William Sound, where they find the last food-rich marine environment before they cross mountain passes to the western and arctic coast.

No wonder that the most important feeding area, the 80-mile-wide Copper River Delta, is considered such a vital link by the Western Hemisphere Shorebird Reserve Network, an international network that identifies and works to protect vital shorebird habitat throughout the western hemisphere. ■

Puffins also congregate more along the outer coast, but a small colony nests in the Dutch Group, on two sea stacks capped with hummocks.

Besides arctic terns, black oystercatchers and other shorebirds and waterfowl nest along beaches and marshes. While the cliff dwellers congregate in large numbers, many shore-nesting birds are less obvious, depending on camouflage for protection. Some, such as the harlequin duck, nest along forest streams, eating freshwater insects while raising their young and then foraging for intertidal organisms the rest of the year.

The vast marshes of the Copper River Delta provide nesting territory for many ducks, geese, and swans, including the largest flying bird, the trumpeter swan. Dusky Canada geese nest almost exclusively on the delta. A subspecies of the Canada goose, their numbers have been declining since the 1964 earthquake raised the land on the delta, making their marshy nesting areas high enough for brown bears and coyotes to prey on their eggs and young.

The water birds of the Sound also congregate at feeding sites. Kittiwakes, gulls, and arctic terns swerve and dip gracefully in front of tidewater glaciers, feeding off aquatic organisms at the face of the calving glaciers. Many birds frequent rocky headlands, where they wait for fish to pass or feed on the rich intertidal life. While kayaking around Green Island in late March, I came to a headland populated by pelagic and double-crested cormorants, harlequin ducks, scoters, and puffins.

Seabirds can also be found along the miles-long bands of floating seaweed and aquatic animals created by converging waters: where outgoing tide meets incoming tide, where freshwater meets seawater, and where winds and currents intersect. These distinct bands provide a feast for gulls, cormorants, pigeon guillemots, and marbled murrelets. On the outer coastline, storm petrels, shearwaters, puffins, and sometimes the rare short-tailed albatross forage.

In late summer, streams laden with spawned-out salmon fill with scavenging gulls, ducks, magpies, ravens, and bald eagles. The lagoon at Picturesque Cove is typical. Gulls and eagles screech, hopping around dying salmon at low tide. Ducks swim

BLACK OYSTERCATCHERS

© Randy Brandon

WALK A BEACH along Prince William Sound and you may be surprised by a pair of black oystercatchers noisily luring you away from their hidden nest or flying in an arc to land just in front of or behind you. Of the 15,000 black oystercatchers worldwide, 10 percent live along the intertidal areas of Prince William Sound year-round. They use the chisel-like tip of their long, orange beaks to pry off mussels and clams and to scrape chitons, limpets, and barnacles from rocks. Although they appear curious about humans, they are highly vulnerable to disturbance and fiercely protect their nests and young. Recent research shows a decline in their numbers from disturbances caused by oil-spill cleanup efforts. ■

offshore, waiting their turn. Where the stream pours into the lagoon, black bears swipe out fish and then scramble back up the steep hillside.

As the fish spawn out and the days shorten, the fall bird migration begins. Diffuse and less hurried, it is less dramatic than spring. Birds pass through from July through November, once again finding respite. Early storms sometimes cause large numbers of

*Dusky Canada geese migrate from Oregon's
Willamette Valley to nest on the delta.*

cranes, geese, and ducks to congregate along the Copper River
Delta. These storms may also drive storm petrels into the fjords of
the Sound.

Some birds stay, using innovative strategies to withstand the
winters. Most gather in larger groups. Thousands of oystercatchers, black turnstones, rock sandpipers, dunlins, and
surfbirds gather along the outer islands, where the water is warmer
and food is more plentiful. Harlequins, scoters, and other waterfowl also gather in protected waters. Ptarmigan remain in the
forest, as do winter finches such as crossbills and redpolls. Some
winters, however, these finches all fly south—what biologists refer

to as "superflights." Amazingly, some birds fly to the Sound for the winter, for the Sound is the most northern embayment that is ice-free year-round. Among these far north breeders are king eiders, buffleheads, and oldsquaw.

The diversity of birds in every season is fragile. While still plentiful, many species have suffered severe declines in the past few decades. The numbers of marbled murrelets have declined by 67 percent since 1972; black-legged kittiwake numbers have similarly declined. About three-quarters of all bird carcasses found after the oil spill were murres. And harlequin ducks, which feed in intertidal areas, still suffer higher than usual deaths in winter. Habitat loss and dangers along the flyway also affect birds that nest in or migrate through Prince William Sound. Such dangers and declines underscore the need to protect vital habitat so that the cliffs, hummocks, beaches, and marshes of the Sound will continue to ring with birdsong in every season. ■

Ethnohistory, Explorers, and Enterprise

Humans have occupied Prince William Sound for thousands of years, but their numbers have risen and fallen as waves of people have come through seeking quick fortune. As John Burroughs said 100 years ago after spending time with prospectors at Orca, near Cordova, "Alaska is full of such adventurers ransacking the land." While many found riches, they left behind a depleted and scarred landscape. The challenge of the Sound has been to find a way to live sustainably within it.

First Inhabitants

The first human inhabitants had a mostly sustainable way of living along the Sound. Chugach Eskimos, originally called *Suqpiaq*, hunted marine mammals from *baidarkas* (kayaks), trapped salmon with weirs at stream mouths, and harvested shellfish, herbs, and berries. Dispersed into 8 tribes throughout the Sound, they periodically warred with one another and their neighbors.

They shared the southeastern Sound with Eyak Indians, Athabascans who likely traveled down the Copper River to inhabit the Copper River Delta. The Eyaks, settling in 2 main villages, Eyak and Alaganik, were primarily land hunters. They hunted bears and mountain goats and fished salmon along the river with spears and

Suqpiaq man in spruce root hat, bone nosepin, and ivory labrets.

NUCHEK

NUCHEK, A VILLAGE SITE on western Hinchinbrook Island, encapsulates the history of the Sound in its own. Reported to be one of the Sound's oldest occupied sites, it had the most abundant and diverse food sources of any Chugach village. The protected embayment also afforded a broad view for detecting incoming war parties.

Explorers, too, found this an ideal port because it was not only protected but also had reliable sailing winds and was within a few miles of the Gulf of Alaska. Beginning with Captain James Cook—who used the Native name for the town rather than renaming it—nearly every explorer anchored near Nuchek. In 1792, Russians built Fort St. Constantine and Helen between Constantine Harbor and Port Etches and established Nuchek as the major trading post on the Sound. Tlingits and Athabascans all came to trade furs. Outside the stockades lined with 9 cannons, Native and mixed-race villages grew. Russian Orthodox priests established a chapel and a Native school.

This heyday of Nuchek waned as sea otter pelts became scarce. Disease, too, took its toll on Nuchek, decimating nearly a quarter of the Native population. When Americans took over the post in 1867, only a few years of fur trade were left. The population dropped from 120 in 1890 to 30 in 1909.

What finally ended Nuchek's trade reign, though, was the shift to mainland interests. With gold and copper discoveries inland and canneries opened at Orca (near Cordova), and with the advent of steam engine vessels, a wind-reliable island port was no longer as

dip nets. A third Native group, the Tlingits, sporadically entered the Sound from Controller Bay and Yakutat, alternately warring and trading. With these 3 major Alaska Native groups converging—Eskimos from the western coast, Athabascan Indians from the Interior, and Northwest Coast Indians from Southeast Alaska—a rich cultural diversity developed.

At first Western contact, about 1,000 Natives lived along the Sound, most of them Chugach. Warring, forced recruitment into sea-otter hunting, changes brought by resource ventures such as the Kennecott Copper Mine, and Western diseases contributed to their near-decimation. Today, only 2 Chugach villages remain:

© Marybeth Holleman

desirable. When Chief Peter Chimivitski died in 1929, his family, the village's last occupants, moved from Nuchek to Cordova.

Sixty-five years later, descendants of Nuchek families returned. Under the guidance of John F. C. Johnson, a Nuchek descendant and Cultural Resource Manager and Director for the Chugach Alaska Corporation, a Native spirit camp began operating at the site of the old village in 1995. The camp is called *Nuuciq,* the original Native name. Now, every summer, Nuchek is a place of spiritual and cultural renewal. Johnson also envisions building a cultural heritage center and historical displays that will preserve and continue Nuchek culture while also attracting tourists, making Nuchek once again a meeting point of cultures. ■

Chenega Bay and Tatitlek. Both Eyak villages are gone, and only one remaining elder still speaks the Eyak language.

The Era of Exploration

About 250 years ago, Europeans from Russia, England, Spain, France, and Portugal began converging on Prince William Sound. They came in search of treasures and trade routes, and left behind their names.

The first European explorer to set anchor in Alaska was Vitus Bering, a Dane leading a Russian expedition in 1741. His ship, the *Saint Peter,* anchored off Kayak Island, where German naturalist

Georg Wilhelm Steller documented plants and animals. Steller's name lives on: the Steller jay, Steller sea lion, and the now-extinct Steller sea cow. The other legacy of Bering's voyage stemmed from the ultrasoft sea otter pelts they brought back—thus igniting the Russian-dominated era of lucrative sea otter hunting.

In the meantime, other European explorers arrived, many searching for the Northwest Passage, a sea route across the continent. Captain James Cook sailed his HMS *Resolution* into Prince William Sound in May 1778. Though the Russians referred to it as "Chugach Bay," he named it "Sandwich Sound," later changing it to "Prince William Sound" after England's crown prince. He also named Montague Island after the patron of his trip, John Montagu of Sandwich, and Hinchinbrook Island after his patron's father. He spent 8 days exploring and repairing his ship at Snug Corner Cove—which he named for its calm anchor—and then sailed to Unalaska, where he told Russian fur traders of the abundant sea otters in the Sound.

Spanish Lieutenant Salvador Fidalgo also arrived in search of the Northwest Passage and explored much of the northeastern Sound, naming Cordova, Port Gravina, and "Puerto de Valdes" after officials in Spain's navy.

The most extensive early exploration was made in 1794 by Captain George Vancouver, who first saw the Sound with Captain Cook. Vancouver's lieutenants, Whidbey and Johnstone, surveyed the eastern and western Sound in small boats. Whidbey named many northwestern places, including Port Wells, Esther Island, Point Culross, Point Pigot, and Passage Canal. Vancouver named Port Fidalgo after the Spanish explorer. Their survey work formed the basis for sailing charts after the United States purchased Alaska in 1867.

While these explorers passed through, Russians established a fur hunting outpost, Fort St. Constantine and Helen, at the Chugach village of Nuchek. From 1783 to 1819, hundreds of Russians, as well as perhaps thousands of Aleut and Koniag, hunted sea otters in the Sound. While the Russians apparently didn't force the Chugach into hunting, the fur trade nonetheless contributed to their decline. Not only did it bring alcohol and disease, but it also created a dependence on the trading posts, weakening the subsistence

"VOYAGE OF DISCOVERY"

WHILE MOST TRAVELED TO PRINCE WILLIAM SOUND looking for quick wealth or new routes, some came only to look. The first of these was the Harriman Expedition of 1899. Comprised of 25 of the nation's best scientists, naturalists, and artists, the expedition spent nearly a month at Prince William Sound studying, photographing, and painting glaciers, flora, and fauna. Their scientific papers provided a baseline for future studies. They also named Columbia Glacier, College Fiord and its glaciers—those on the west for women's colleges, those on the east for men's colleges—and Harriman Glacier and Fiord, which they discovered. John Muir, trip naturalist, described their approach to Barry Glacier and their discovery:

"As we approached the head of one of the Prince William Sound fjords, it seemed to be completely blocked by the front of a large glacier and an outreaching headland. The local pilot, turning to our Captain Doran, said: 'Here, take your ship. I am not going to be responsible for her if she is to be run into every unsounded, uncharted channel and frog marsh.' The Captain slowed down, and in a few minutes stopped, after creeping forward to within half a mile or so of the front of the ice wall.

"Then Mr. Harriman asked me if I was satisfied with what I had seen and was ready to turn back, to which I replied: 'Judging from the trends of this fjord and glacier, there must be a corresponding fjord or glacier to the southward, and although the ship has probably gone as far as it is safe to go, I wish you would have a boat lowered and let me take a look around that headland into the hidden half of the landscape.'

"'We can perhaps run the ship there,' he said, and immediately ordered the captain to 'go ahead and try to pass between the ice wall and headland.' The passage was dangerously narrow and threatening, but gradually opened into a magnificent icy fjord about twelve miles long, stretching away to the southward. The water continuing deep, as the soundline showed, Mr. Harriman quietly ordered the captain to go right ahead up the middle of the new fjord. 'Full speed, sir?' inquired the captain. 'Yes, full speed ahead.' The sail up this majestic fjord in the evening sunshine, picturesquely varied glaciers coming successively to thundering wave-raising icebergs, was, I think, the most exciting experience of the whole trip." ■

An abandoned gold mine along Valdez Arm.

economy. Because of intermarriages and conversions to the Russian Orthodox Church, many Natives now have Russian names and consider themselves more Aleut than Chugach.

Waves of Fortune

The Russians may have been the first in search of wealth, but they weren't the last. From the last decade of the 1800s to the mid-1900s, Westerners pulsed through Prince William Sound looking to make their fortunes in gold, copper, fur farming, and fishing. These early ventures were marked by short-lived wealth and rapid resource exploitation that mirror the economic history of the entire state.

During the winter and spring of 1897–98, more than 4,000 people flooded through Valdez to attempt the all-American route to the Klondike gold fields. Unprepared for the glacier cross-ings and subzero temperatures, most never made it to the Klondike. Some stayed and searched for minerals. As claims ran into the several thousands, complex mining operations sprouted from the Sound's cliffs and coves. One, the Ruff and Tuff Gold Mine, was actually on a *nunatuk*—a sawtooth peak rising above an ice field—in the middle of the Columbia Glacier.

Prospectors found gold to the northwest and copper to the southeast of Valdez. The largest gold mine was the Cliff Mine in Port Valdez; its remains were washed away by the 1964 earthquake. The second largest, the Granite Mine, lies along Port Wells. Peaking in 1922, it was worked sporadically until the early 1960s. Rusty remains are evident along Port Wells and in Harrison Lagoon; the hillsides surrounding the lagoon were clearcut for the mine.

The largest copper find was at LaTouche. At its height between 1903 and 1928, it supported a town of nearly 3,000 people. Its collapsing remains still scar the mountainside across from Chenega Bay. The Kennecott Copper Mine, though it was inland nearly 200 miles, nonetheless profoundly affected Prince William Sound. After its discovery in 1900, a railroad was built from Orca Inlet, establishing the town of Cordova. Operating for 27 years, it was the largest copper mine of its day.

The first commercial oil discovery in Alaska also was adjacent to Prince William Sound, along the shores, Controller Bay. In 1894, prospector Tom White slipped in a black puddle and discovered the Katalla oil site, where 154,000 barrels of oil were extracted over a period of 29 years.

A few prospectors turned to fox farming. Many more joined them when, in 1913, blue fox furs suddenly became fashionable. By 1925, 34 islands in the Sound contained foxes. Farmers would release pairs on an island, where they would run wild, eating birds and small rodents as well as salmon placed in feed houses by the farmers. Fashions changed and profit dropped a decade later, and now the foxes are gone. But along the shores of some islands you can see the rotting remains of feed houses. Some islands, such as Bald Head Chris and Axel Lind, carry the names of the farmers.

The resource that's still lucrative—fisheries—also got its start at the turn of the century, but it wasn't until the beginning of World War I that enough demand was created to fuel a wave of canneries. In the 1920s, canneries bought salmon from purse-seining boats and collected their own from fish traps. These traps were abhorred by fishermen because the traps could catch nearly an entire run of salmon and wipe out the stock. Some fishermen became "fish pirates": they would steal the fish from the traps and then sell them to the canneries. With little or no regulation, canneries continued to exploit both the resource and cheap labor by importing poor immigrants. Not surprisingly, the salmon population crashed in the 1940s and 1950s. With statehood, fish traps were outlawed and working conditions improved, but by the 1960s, most runs were so small that canneries closed anyhow. You can find the remains of canneries at many sites, including Port Nellie Juan and Knight Island.

Not all came seeking quick fortune. With the gold prospectors came government expeditions to survey and map routes. Captain William R. Abercrombie, who was in Valdez during the chaotic winter of the Klondike 98ers, pioneered a route to the Interior through Lowe River and Thompson Pass that later became the foundation of the Richardson Highway. The U.S. Bureau of Fisheries sent Samuel Applegate in 1887; he named Port Nellie Juan after his schooner. Another government expedition, led by Captain E. F. Glenn, surveyed the Portage Pass route to Cook Inlet.

Recent Enterprise

The latest boom is the crude oil flowing from Alaska's North Slope down the 800-mile trans-Alaska pipeline to Valdez, where it is loaded on tankers that lumber down Valdez Arm and out Hinchinbrook Entrance. Completed in 1977, the pipeline has changed Prince William Sound, both in its economic impact on Valdez and Alaska and in its environmental destruction and degradation. But it, too, may someday be only an historical remnant. The Kennecott Copper Mine operated nearly 30 years; the pipeline may carry oil only that long as well.

In the last decade, Alaska Native corporations have clearcut large swaths of old-growth forest, primarily on Montague Island and along the eastern Sound near Cordova and Tatitlek. The scars of these clearcuts will remain for at least 100 years, for this most-northern temperate rain forest is more slow-growing than the rest of the Pacific Northwest.

Today, other economic activity centers around salmon and tourism, both potentially sustainable economies. Since 1974, 5 pink salmon hatcheries have been built on the Sound to supple-

FISHING BOATS

MOST COMMERCIAL FISHING BOATS you'll see on the Sound during summer months are catching salmon or halibut. Longliners fish for halibut from 30- to 50-foot vessels. On their decks you'll see a line hauler and dozens of tubs holding the hooks and lines; flagpoles with orange flags mark their "sets" of lines.

Purse seiners use 2 boats: a 38- to 58-foot vessel with a large boom extending over the back deck and 2 smaller booms off to either side, and a small skiff. The skiff runs a wall of net out from the boat, either around a school of fish or open along a cape. The net is then closed at the bottom, making a "purse" that is hauled in with a power block hanging from the boom.

Bowpickers or sternpickers are used by drift gillnetters in the northwestern Sound and along the Copper River Delta. The 26- to 32-foot boats have a net reel on the bow or stern from which the 900-foot-long wall of net is attached, spun out, and then reeled back in. Skiffs are used by set gillnetters along beaches, mostly in Maine and Eshamy Bays. One end of the net is attached to the beach, and the other end is set out with the skiff.

Tenders are the biggest commercial fishing boats you'll see: these 60- to 100-foot boats can carry 100,000 pounds of fish. Fishing vessels deliver their catches to the tender, which then transports fish to shore-based processors. ■

---

ment wild stocks. Other commercial fisheries target halibut, black cod, and herring. In the last 2 decades, a few people have begun oyster farming in protected bays. Guided tourism also began in the early 1970s, and cruise ships began arriving in the early 1980s. Tourism will grow exponentially with the opening of the road between Whittier and Portage.

For nearly 300 years now, non-Native people have availed themselves of Prince William Sound's treasures, most often with little regard for long-term impact. Still, the Sound feels wild and untrammeled in many places. It's this wildness that the nonhuman inhabitants depend upon, and that we human visitors so appreciate. The task for us in the future is to learn how to be in this place, enjoying its abundances, without decimating them. ■

Hard Aground—
The <u>Exxon Valdez</u>

What we see now is death. Death, not of each other but of the source of life—the water.... It is too shocking to understand. Never in the millennium of our tradition have we thought it possible for the water to die. But it is true.

—Walter Meganak, Aleut elder, June 1989

On March 24, 1989, just after midnight, the tanker *Exxon Valdez*, carrying 1.3 million barrels of oil, struck Bligh Reef in Valdez Arm. During the next few days, more than 40,000 tons of crude oil flowed from the punctured tanker, making this the largest oil spill ever in North America. This manmade disaster occurred exactly 25 years after the Sound's last natural disaster, the great earthquake of 1964.

The recipe for this disaster began with the discovery of oil in the Beaufort Sea's Prudhoe Bay. Throughout the debates on how the oil should be transported, the Sound's fishing communities lobbied for an overland route because they feared the effects of an oil spill.

Though many safeguards were promised, most were never established. There were few double-hulled tankers; the spill response plan was inadequate and equipment meager; and the

A decade after the spill, the Sound's waters are clear, but ecosystem effects continue.

Coast Guard's vessel traffic system radar couldn't observe tankers as far out as Bligh Reef.

After 3 days, winds picked up and pushed the oil slick south across the extremely productive, pristine, cold-water, protected shores of Prince William Sound. It couldn't have happened at a worse time: herring were moving near shore to spawn, migratory seabirds and whales were returning, juvenile salmon were emerging from streams, harbor seals and sea otters were pupping, or preparing to, and the spring plankton bloom had just begun. The spill eventually spread over more than 10,000 square miles of Alaska's coastal ocean, oiling over 1,500 miles of some of the world's wildest coastline and making this the world's most destructive oil spill ever.

Initial effects were devastating. More marine mammals and seabirds were killed directly by oil than in any manmade disaster ever. The estimates are numbing: 22 killer whales, 200 harbor seals, up to 6,000 sea otters, 700,000 seabirds. Some murre colonies lost up to 75 percent of their breeding population. That year's offspring of herring was essentially lost, as were several years' offspring of pink salmon. Terrestrial mammals were found oiled and killed—deer, brown bears, mink, river otters.

Though the Exxon Corporation spent $2 billion in a massive cleanup effort that turned the once-quiet Sound into an industrial zone with more than 10,000 workers and 1,000 vessels, less than 10 percent of the oil was recovered. And though thousands volunteered in makeshift wildlife recovery efforts, most animals died even after they were cleaned of the toxic oil. The lesson has been, as one fisherman and marine biologist said, "Once you've spilled it, you've lost."

Having learned the lesson the hard way, government agencies and the consortium of oil companies have made many improvements in spill prevention and response. Now, 2 Coast Guard tugs escort every loaded tanker out of the Sound; now, Coast Guard radar tracks all tankers while they're in the Sound. There are, however, still no new double-hulled tankers, and some think the risks are even greater today because the ships are a decade older.

Lines of booms attempt to contain an oil slick in April 1989.

Two years after the spill, the natural resource damage suit was settled out of court, and Exxon paid $1 billion to the state and federal governments. With this, the state and federal governments set up the *Exxon Valdez* Oil Spill (EVOS) Trustee Council, composed of state and federal representatives, to use the money for restoration. Most of the money has been spent on research and habitat acquisition. However, other than habitat protection, the Trustee Council could do little to restore the spill area. As its science coordinator said, "Most restoration has and will continue to occur through natural processes."

Reverberating effects have continued. Sea otters were essentially exterminated from the southwestern Sound. In their absence,

HABITAT PROTECTION: A SILVER LINING

© Karen Jettmar

MARBLED MURRELETS fish in Prince William Sound's salt water, but they nest on horizontal mats of moss high in the arms of old-growth spruce and hemlock. For them, both forest and sea are vital. It's true for many other species that were injured by the spill as well—many use the land to nest, feed, molt, overwinter, and find shelter. Even salmon need clear-running, unobstructed streams shaded by towering old-growth forests.

Protecting these forests from clearcutting and other habitat-damaging activity is critical to assisting in the recovery of these animals. To this end, the habitat acquisition program of the EVOS (*Exon Valdez* Oil Spill) Trustee Council has purchased title or conservation easements to 205,000 acres of coastal rain forest bordering Prince William Sound, protecting 175 salmon streams and 600 miles of shoreline. All were purchased from Native corporations, some of which had resorted to clearcutting to make a profit; instead, the corporations make a profit and the trees stand. Most of these lands, located on southwestern and eastern Prince William Sound, help complete the ecosystem managed as the Chugach National Forest. ■

sea urchins proliferated and have decimated kelp forests, upon which a host of subtidal life depends. Herring populations collapsed for the first time on record in 1993, succumbing to a viral disease, and have yet to return in prespill numbers. Their loss affects the entire ecosystem, for they are a keystone species— principal prey for more than 40 other species, including seabirds, seals, sea lions, whales, and fish. Twenty-two members of one resident pod of killer whales disappeared in the 8 years immediately following the spill. In addition, some members split off and now travel with another pod—a behavior unprecedented in killer-whale biology.

Ten years and billions of dollars of cleanup and restoration later, oil still lurks beneath the surface of many beaches in southwestern Prince William Sound. Studies have shown it to still be highly toxic—"like a minefield," said one biologist. And, of 23 species identified as injured, only 2 have recovered: bald eagles and river otters. More than half are still listed as not recovering or recovery unknown.

Overall, recovery will continue to be slow and incomplete. But there's one effect we can mitigate. The oil spill brought Prince William Sound to the world's attention, and, after the first couple of years, tourist visitation skyrocketed. With the road to Whittier, visitor numbers will continue to climb. Through attention to our impacts on this fragile and wild place, we can help lessen future harm. ◼

Today's Communities

Today, 5 communities cling to the shores between mountains and sea along Prince William Sound. All have weathered the 1964 earthquake, the 1989 oil spill, and myriad economic booms and busts.

Cordova, situated among mountains, water, and the vast Copper River Delta, began in 1906 as the rail terminus for the Kennecott Copper Mine. It outlived the mine through a developing fishery; now it's an important U.S. fishing port. Cordovans harvest world-famous Copper River red salmon, as well as herring, pink salmon, and bottomfish. In early May, they host the Copper River Delta Shorebird Festival, as birders from around the world flock to see the millions of shorebirds passing through on their spring migrations. The 2,500 residents also celebrate the Ice Worm Festival, a weekend-long anti–cabin-fever event in early February.

Tatitlek is a Native community of more than 100 people located on the mainland between Port Fidalgo and Valdez Arm. Here, as at Chenega Bay, residents depend on subsistence hunting, fishing, and gathering. Residents also work at commercial fishing and an expanding oyster farm.

Ice Worm Festival fireworks illuminate Cordova's boat harbor, which holds most of the Sound's commercial fleet.

Commercial fishers haul a salmon seine aboard.

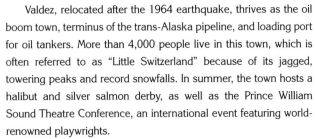

Valdez, relocated after the 1964 earthquake, thrives as the oil boom town, terminus of the trans-Alaska pipeline, and loading port for oil tankers. More than 4,000 people live in this town, which is often referred to as "Little Switzerland" because of its jagged, towering peaks and record snowfalls. In summer, the town hosts a halibut and silver salmon derby, as well as the Prince William Sound Theatre Conference, an international event featuring world-renowned playwrights.

Whittier's tourist center sells a button that reads: "Whittier Rain Festival: 365 Days a Year." If you spend any time here, it's easy to see why the military established it as a supply port in World War II: before radar, it was a good place to hide. Clouds, winds, and rain collect at the end of Passage Canal—but so do tour boats, charters, and recreational boats. It's the port of entry

▲ © Debra Mercy

© Alissa Crandall

Ready-for-market farmed oysters are harvested at Tatitlek.

for most visitors to the Sound, as well as for freight, providing the only barge-rail connection in the state. It's still a small town; only about 300 people live here year-round. But all this may soon change. The new road linking Whittier with the Seward Highway at Portage is expected to increase visitation from 200,000 a year to nearly 2 million.

Chenega Bay, the Sound's other remaining Native village, is like a phoenix resurrecting in the face of disaster. The 1964 earthquake literally wiped out the village, with survivors moving to Tatitlek, Cordova, and Anchorage. But with determination and vision, the town regrouped and rebuilt on Evans Island. Then, 25 years after the earthquake, disaster struck again in the form of the 1989 oil spill. Chenega Bay's part of the Sound was the hardest hit, threatening its subsistence way of life. In the past 8 years, the population has fallen from about 100 to only 35.

Each of these towns has developed unique economic and social characteristics. Yet whether they depend on subsistence, commercial fishing, tourism, or oil, they are all alike in one basic way: as goes the health of Prince William Sound, so go these communities.

▶ © Marybeth Holleman

~

Prince William Sound provides more than 100 million pounds of fish each year; 20 percent of the nation's domestically produced oil is shipped through its complex marine ecosystem; claims and development plans for mineral deposits are on the upswing again; and tourism, especially on the western side, is burgeoning, with dozens of permit requests for floating lodges, fuel docks, and other visitor amenities.

Residents and resource managers are now asking, What is the carrying capacity of Prince William Sound? How many people can it support and in what ways? What is the best path to ensure sustainable communities?

In this enchanted circle born of ice and rock, there's a unique diversity of landscape and wildlife at stake. From the vast ice fields to the intricate intertidal zones, from the millions of migrating birds to the massive humpback whales, from the mighty brown and reclusive black bears to the millions of returning salmon on which

A view of Harrison Lagoon from a U.S. Forest Service cabin.

they feast, from the web of rain forests to the deep fjords, the Sound is still a place where nature reigns. But it will take far-reaching vision and commitment for us to protect the wild inhabitants and ensure that the enchanted circle remains unbroken. ◼

Recommended Reading

Alaska Geographic Society. *Prince William Sound.* Anchorage, 1993.

Arctic Environmental and Information Data Center. *A Field Guide to Prince William Sound.* Anchorage: University of Alaska, 1991.

Armstrong, Robert H. *Alaska's Fish: A Guide to Selected Species.* Seattle: Alaska Northwest Books, 1996.

————. *Guide to the Birds of Alaska.* Seattle: Alaska Northwest Books, 1998.

Banko, Winston E. *The Trumpeter Swan.* Lincoln: University of Nebraska Press, 1980.

Burroughs, John, John Muir, and George Grinnell. *Harriman Alaska Expedition, Alaska: Vol 1.* London: John Murray, 1902.

Carson, Rachel. *The Edge of the Sea.* New York: Houghton Mifflin, 1955.

De Laguna, Frederica. *Chugach Prehistory: The Archaeology of Prince William Sound.* Seattle: University of Washington Press, 1956.

Exxon Valdez Oil Spill Trustee Council. *Legacy of an Oil Spill: 10 Years After Exxon Valdez.* Anchorage: EVOS Trustee Council, 1999.

Fairchild, Jill, ed. *Trees: A Celebration.* New York: Weidenfeld & Nicolson, 1989.

Field, Carmen, and Conrad Field. *Alaska's Seashore Creatures: A Guide to Selected Marine Invertebrates.* Seattle: Alaska Northwest Books, 1999.

Ford, Corey. *Where the Sea Breaks Its Back: The Epic Story of Early Naturalist Georg Steller and the Russian Exploration of Alaska.* Seattle: Alaska Northwest Books, 1992.

Isleib, M. E., and Brina Kessel. *Birds of the North Gulf Coast—Prince William Sound Region, Alaska.* Biological Papers of the University of Alaska, 1973. Fairbanks: University of Alaska Press, 1989.

Johnson, John F. C. *Chugach Legends.* Anchorage: Chugach Alaska Corporation, 1984.

Lethcoe, Jim. *Geology of Prince William Sound, Alaska.* Valdez: Prince William Sound Books, 1990.

Lethcoe, Jim, and Nancy Lethcoe. *Cruising Guide to Prince William Sound.* Valdez: Prince William Sound Books, 1984.

————. *A History of Prince William Sound, Alaska.* Valdez: Prince William Sound Books, 1994.

Lethcoe, Nancy. *Glaciers of Prince William Sound, Alaska.* Valdez: Prince William Sound Books, 1987.

Matkin, Craig. *The Killer Whales of Prince William Sound.* Valdez: Prince William Sound Books, 1994.

Michelson, Pete. *Natural History of Alaska's Prince William Sound.* Cordova: Alaska Wild Wings, 1989.

Muir, John. *Edward Henry Harriman.* Coastal Parks Association, 1978.

Romano-Lax, Andromeda. *How to Rent a Public Cabin in Southcentral Alaska.* Berkeley, California: Wilderness Press, 1999.

Schofield, Janice J. *Discovering Wild Plants: Alaska, Western Canada, The Northwest.* Seattle: Alaska Northwest Books, 1989.

Smith, Dave. *Alaska's Mammals: A Guide to Selected Species.* Seattle: Alaska Northwest Books, 1995.

Wynne, Kate. *Guide to Marine Mammals of Alaska.* Anchorage: Alaska Sea Grant College Program, University of Alaska, 1993.

INDEX

*Page numbers in **bold face** indicate photos.*

Alaska Northwest Books is proud to publish another book in its Alaska Pocket Guide series, designed with the curious traveler in mind. Ask for more books in this series at your favorite bookstore, or contact Alaska Northwest Books™.

ALASKA NORTHWEST BOOKS™

An imprint of Graphic Arts Center Publishing Company
P.O. Box 10306, Portland, OR 97296-0306
503-226-2402; www.gacpc.com